Brimming with creative inspiration, how-to projects, and useful information to enrich your everyday life, Quarto Knows is a favorite destination for those pursuing their interests and passions. Visit our site and dig deeper with our books into your area of interest: Quarto Creates, Quarto Cooks, Quarto Homes, Quarto Lives, Quarto Drives, Quarto Explores, Quarto Gifts, or Quarto Kids.

Inspiring | Educating | Creating | Entertaining

24 23 22 21 20   1 2 3 4 5

ISBN: 978-0-7603-6604-2

Digital edition published in 2020
eISBN: 978-0-7603-6605-9

The information in this book previously appeared in *Success with Succulents* by John Bagnasco and Bob Reidmuller (Cool Springs Press, 2017).

Library of Congress Cataloging-in-Publication Data

Names: Bagnasco, John, author. | Reidmuller, Robert, Jr., 1953- author.
Title: Success with succulents : choosing, growing, and caring for cactuses and other succulents / John Bagnasco, Robert Reidmuller, Jr.
Description: Minneapolis, MN : Cool Springs Press, 2017. | Includes index.
Identifiers: LCCN 2017022970 | ISBN 9780760353585 (sc with flaps)
Subjects: LCSH: Succulent plants.
Classification: LCC SB438 .B246 2017 | DDC 635.9/525—dc23
LC record available at https://lccn.loc. gov/2017022970

Design: Laura Shaw Design
Cover Image: Shutterstock

Photography by Rebecca Eichten except as noted otherwise.

Printed in China

PHOTO CREDITS
ALAMY: 112 top (Universal Images Group North America LLC/DeAgostini), 119 top (National Geographic Creative), 180 bottom (Florapix), 195 top (Alan Gregg), 197 bottom (Alan Gregg)
ALTMAN PLANTS: 92–93, 139 bottom, 174 top
BOB REIDMULLER: 102, 104 top, 106 bottom, 120, 126, 132, 134, 138 top, 144 both, 148–149, 162 bottom, 168 top, 191 bottom, 198 both
C. T. JOHANSSON/WIKIMEDIA: 116 bottom
DAKE~COMMONSWIKI/WIKIMEDIA: 179 bottom
SHUTTERSTOCK: 1, 23 top, 27, 48 bottom right, 101, 170 bottom, 172 top, 192 top row and bottom right, 196 bottom, 202

MIX
Paper from responsible sources
FSC® C008047

Succulents

choosing, growing,
and caring for
cactuses and
other succulents

JOHN BAGNASCO & BOB REIDMULLER

COOL
SPRINGS
PRESS

Contents

Featured Plants   100 Top Choices of Cactuses and Succulents

INTRODUCTION

More Than Hens and Chicks

*J*t once was the case that when most people thought of succulents for the home, they thought of "Aunt Jenny's jade plant." But the ubiquitous jade, *Crassula ovata*, is just the beginning of a limitless array of varieties of tough plants available to indoor and outdoor gardeners. Because they are beautiful, unique, and nearly indestructible if not overwatered, cactuses and other succulents are exploding in popularity. In areas of unreliable water availability, like the Southwest, a wide selection of sizes and striking architectural features add interest and excitement to both home and commercial landscapes.

So, while cactuses and succulents have captivated the botanical community for several centuries, their versatility has now ensconced them into the trendiness of the twenty-first-century plant scene. Hens and chicks, *Sempervivum* spp., have been perennial favorites for years in climates as cold as northern Montana and are presently available in more than three thousand cultivars. Today, the emergence of online shopping has helped hobbyists around the country gain access to more exotic succulents that, though not cold hardy, are happy to spend summers outside and over-winter indoors. Although tender leafy plants are often damaged during

. . . .

(OPPOSITE) Unusual and attractive curly leaf *Agave*.

shipping, succulents are advantageously equipped to withstand shipment abuse and arrive unscathed at their destinations.

Both the popularity of container gardening and online marketing have skyrocketed the popularity of succulents, elevating the humdrum world of hens and chicks and other prosaic perennials into stylish plant swank. This trend is here to stay as environmentally conscious gardeners remake their corners of the planet.

SUCCULENTS OUTSIDE AND IN

Indoor plant enthusiasts often daydream about the "ideal" houseplant: something that comes in interesting shapes, has attractive flowers, can withstand the low humidity of winter indoors, thrives with minimal care, and still evokes gasps of admiration from visitors. By these criteria, the "ideal" plant is a succulent. The emergence of cell phone technology has allowed millennials, in particular, to be credited with boosting succulent popularity. The main reason? Succulents look great on camera. The hashtag #succulents has over six million posts on Instagram alone!

(left) Gasteraloe in a rock garden.

. . . .

(OPPOSITE) Echeveria hybrid with emerging inflorescence.

. . . .

(NEXT SPREAD) A beautiful black and silver dyckia.

Generally, succulents are water-thrifty plants that are adapted to dry environments in which the leaves, stems, or roots have become unusually fleshy from the development of water-storing tissue. Plants adapted to living in dry environments, such as succulents, are known as xerophytes—from the Greek *xero* (dry) and *phyton* (plant). However, not all xerophytes are succulents, because there are other ways of adapting to a shortage of water, such as by developing small leaves that may roll up or by having leathery rather than succulent leaves. Nor are all succulents xerophytes, because plants like swamp stonecrop, *Crassula helmsii*, are both succulent and aquatic.

Succulents come in a plethora of styles, sizes, and colors. With so many varieties available, the authors hope that this book can be used as a simple yet comprehensive reference tool for growing succulents, with tips on watering, fertilizing, and basic maintenance. Succulent growing can be addictive, and if you are not careful, you are likely to get "hooked" (especially when handling cactuses)!

What Are Cactuses?
What Are Succulents?

*J*f you're new to these plants, you might be a bit confused by the terms *cactus* and *succulent*. But there is a simple mantra you can remember: all cactuses are succulents, but not all succulents are cactuses. Although both are succulents (from the Latin *succulentus,* meaning "sap" or "juice") and store moisture in their roots, stems, and/or leaves, the pickle is in the prickle!

Specifically, cactuses are equipped with a special organ called an areole that is responsible for several things. This includes the creation of branches or stems, flowers, fruits, spines, and, believe it or not, even true leaves in some members. But it is the areole-born spine that sets cactuses apart from all other succulents. Cactus spines produced from areoles are akin to human hair or fingernails—they are nonvascular, are not alive, and there is nothing in them that will leak out.

Areoles are easy to spot because they look like small round or oval fuzzy buttons, but woe be to those who are fooled. Aside from the obvious large spines on many cactuses in the subfamily *Opuntioideae* (which one would obviously avoid touching), there is a second line of defense on the areole itself. Small, sometimes not easily visible, modified spines

(OPPOSITE) Beautiful succulent dish gardens.

known as glochids lurk at the base of the larger spines. They can detach very easily and can cause an annoying, lingering irritation to the skin and are not easily extricated. They have an extra punch of being so small and light as to become airborne and find their way into the eyes, mouth, or nostrils. It is often far less debilitating to be jabbed with a large barbed spine that can be easily (albeit painfully) seen and removed.

In non-cactus succulents, on the other hand, spines—or, more correctly, thorns—are vascular in nature, meaning they have arisen from the surface of the plant as a modification of the skin and are a living extension of that plant's tissues. Inside, they have sap or juice just like the rest of the plant, which you can easily see by snipping one with some shears. Not only will moist tissue be visible, but also in many cases it will ooze liquid, or "bleed."

(ABOVE) Watch out for glochids—the little spines can cause disproportionate irritation if they get lodged in your skin.

(OPPOSITE) Areoles are one of the distinguishing features of cactuses.

✽ Spines, Thorns, and Prickles

In everyday English, these three terms are often used interchangeably, but scientifically they actually refer to different structures. Keep in mind that in the hundreds of thousands of members of the plant kingdom there will be some exceptions to the information here, but the general overview is this:

✽ Cactuses have **spines** of various forms, purposes, and appearances. They are usually barbed, causing them to work deeper and deeper into whatever they touch. They are nonvascular, not living, defense mechanisms.

✽ Non-cactus succulents and many other families of plants have **thorns** (though more often, but incorrectly, called spines). Thorns are living vascular extensions of the plant's tissue and are not typically barbed. Some succulents, such as agaves and yuccas, have at the very tip of their leaves what is referred to as an apical spine, but as previously explained, it is physiologically a thorn.

✽ The third well-known example of pointed plant protection has been so wrong in everyday speech for so long that its correct name is mostly known only to rosarians. Contrary to popular belief, roses and members of the rose family (like the blackberry and other brambles) don't actually have thorns! They have **prickles**. It is not unusual for people to say they have been pricked by a rose, and centuries of literature are peppered with fair maidens who have pricked their delicate fingers on this classic flower. This clearly explains why one's finger is "pricked" and not "thorned."

Cactuses are a classic part of the landscape in the American Southwest.

CACTACEAE: THE CACTUS FAMILY

Cactuses are recognized around the world as iconic symbols of the American Southwest, thanks primarily to cinema and television images. However, such superstars as the giant saguaro (*Carnegiea gigantea*) and the golden barrel (*Echinocactus grusonii*) represent just a morsel of a much longer and older history. There are easily more than two centuries of studies, papers, and treatises as well as ongoing and ever-changing research and discovery regarding cactuses. It is our intention to give a broad overview of this group for the purposes of general familiarization and to encourage you to do further research of more detailed scientific and theoretical information.

Cactuses, defined as members of the succulent family Cactaceae, are native only to the New World. Over time, they evolved and spread, covering the Americas from Patagonia, the southern tip of South America, all the way north into western Canada. With this broad establishment eventually came a survival diversity of immense proportions. Some adapted to freezing, snow-covered plains in the lowlands of North America as well as chilling, rocky surroundings at extreme altitudes in mountainous regions like the Andes. At the other end of the survival spectrum are the searing deserts with inhuman temperatures and minimal to nearly immeasurable rainfall. And not to be left out, the hot, humid, and rainy jungles of Central America and the

rainforests of South America have their seemingly un-cactus-like exotic versions.

The majority of the tropical types have taken to living as epiphytes—species that climb or hang on other plants. Some epiphyte cactuses are long clumps of pendent stems beginning from seeds deposited high in the forest canopy by birds and other cactus-fruit-eating creatures, or bits of existing plants that break off and find a suitable branch to anchor onto.

In all of this diversity, native cultures for well over a thousand years have used, and still use, various types of cactuses for food, medicine, shelter, and religious practices.

Because of this diversity, the taxonomists who diligently investigate and classify all things living on the planet have *up to this point* settled on four subfamilies in the main family Cactaceae: Pereskioideae, Opuntioideae, Maihuenioideae, and Cactoideae. In the past, plant characteristics and families were obtained and decided by physical observations of the naked eye. Today, electron microscopes and other tools reduce things down to a cellular level to reveal differences that the naked eye cannot. The following list is a breakdown showing these four subfamilies and *some* of the representative genera that belong to each one that the reader is more likely to come across in cultivation. This is in no way a totally inclusive list, just a general reference to help understand the group.

(ABOVE) Pereskioideae; (BOTTOM) Opuntiodeae; (OPPOSITE) Sedum 'Burrito' spilling out of a mixed succulent planter.

Pereskioideae

GENUS: *Pereskia*

There is only one genus in the Pereskioideae subfamily, *Pereskia*, which comprises approximately 17 species. These species are tropical in nature, and considered to be the oldest group— the first cactuses. These are vining, woody-stemmed plants that are generally considered to be non-succulent. They are the only members of the cactus family that have regular, persistent leaves (which are semi-succulent in some species) and flowers that look like a single-flower species of rose. But how can woody stems, real leaves, and non-succulent properties equate to cactuses? One feature belies the family connection: in the axil above each petiole (leaf stalk) where it attaches to the vining stem is an areole with full-on proper spines, the cactus birth certificate.

Opuntioideae

GENERA: *Opuntia, Austrocylindropuntia, Brasiliopuntia, Cylindropuntia, Consolea, Tephrocactus*

The opuntioids generally consist of two recognizable forms—the round or oval-shaped flattened pads of the "prickly pear" or "beavertail" types and the cylindrical, jointed stems most often seen in the "cholla" and cane types. In the beginning of each growing season, some opuntias develop small, finger-like, cylindrical leaves that are fleshy and highly succulent.

Maihuenioideae

GENUS: *Maihuenia*

Maihuenia, the only genus in this subfamily, includes two species that are rarely found in cultivation. The *Maihuenia* species are low-growing, cushion-forming cactuses native to the higher elevations of the Andes mountains in Argentina and Chile. They produce short, cylindrical stems with small, fleshy, finger-like succulent leaves similar to the opuntias, but these are persistent, aiding in photosynthesis.

Cactoideae

GENERA: *Browningia, Stetsonia, Astrophytum, Echinocactus, Ferocactus, Leuchtenbergia, Mammillaria, Stenocactus, Schlumbergera, Cleistocactus, Espostoa, Gymnocalycium, Oreocereus, Rebutia, Pachycereus*, and more

This is the largest subfamily and accounts for more than 90 different genera that range in size from a centimeter tall to 60 feet (18.3 m) plus. Body shapes are generally round and globular (see photo opposite) or columnar and branched. The trailing, climbing, and hanging jungle cactuses are included in this group as well.

Cultural Uses

Indigenous groups of the Americas have long used various types of cactuses for many purposes. Here are some notable examples.

Opuntia ficus-indica (Indian fig)
The edible fruits of this cactus, commonly known in Spanish as *tuna*, have a sweet taste similar to watermelon, and are eaten fresh or can be processed into jams and jellies. The young tender pads called *nopales* are cooked and prepared various ways as a vegetable. Around 1890, Luther Burbank created the variety 'Burbank's Spineless', primarily as an alternative cattle fodder.

Cereus peruvianus/C. repandus (Peruvian apple)
This columnar cactus produces large, red, spineless fruits that are delicious and refreshing. They are similar to the larger dragon fruit produced by the jungle cactus *Hylocereus undatus*.

Nopalea cochenillifera (nopal cactus)
This *Opuntia* type was used as a host for the female cochineal insect *(Dactylopius coccus)*. Cochineal, a crimson dye, is processed from the body of this insect, which is collected from the cactus. Cochineal dye was used by the Aztec and Mayan peoples of Central and North America for coloring textiles. Though mostly replaced by synthetic dyes today, it is still used for various purposes, including the manufacture of lipstick.

Stenocereus gummosus (Pitahaya agria)
The stems of this cactus were crushed and thrown into lakes and ponds by natives. Substances in the cactus would paralyze the fish, and once they floated to the top were readily gathered by the locals.

Trichocereus pachanoi (San Pedro cactus) and *Lophophora williamsii* (peyote)
Both cactuses contain psychoactive, hallucinogenic compounds capable of inducing visions. These were used in many religious practices and tribal ceremonies.

A rainbow planting of sedums and sedum hybrids.

. . . .

(RIGHT) A climbing aloe variety with a soothing powder-blue glow.

NON-CACTUS SUCCULENTS

While cactuses are categorized under just four subfamilies in the single family Cactaceae, non-cactus succulents are a huge group comprising approximately thirty families. This number is argued to be higher depending on the ever-changing reclassifications.

Here is a partial list of the more typically encountered genera that can be found within those families because a genus is relatively immune to being changed:

Aloe	Frithia	Nolina
Bijlia	Gasteria	Orbea
Bursera	Greenovia	Oscularia
Cissus	Haworthia	Plumeria
Crassula	Huernia	Rosularia
Dudleya	Kalanchoe	Sedum
Echeveria	Lithops	Titanopsis
Euphorbia	Manfreda	Yucca
Faucaria	Monanthes	

The Impostors, Invisibles, and Tricksters

These are often referred to as "mimicry" plants because of their fascinating disguises and abilities to mimic their surroundings. By far the most recognizable are those of the genus *Lithops*. Often referred to as "living stones," these amazing plants have two fleshy lobes with a cleft between them and nearly flat tops, usually decorated in various random markings in earth-toned colors. They "disappear" by disguising themselves as the pebbles around them, which not only protects them but also makes them invisible to grazing animals looking to quench their thirst. Along with *Lithops*, there are other genera that survive by the same or similar means, such as the split rocks (*Pleiospilos*), baby toes (*Fenestraria*), and tiger jaws (*Faucaria*). Also, not typically given common names (other than possibly the generic "stone plants") are *Aloinopsis* and *Titanopsis*. A shared characteristic of many in this group is a "window" at the tips of the lobe-type leaves, or a series of many small-type windows across the leaf surface. With the body of the plants buried in their surroundings, these transparent or translucent windows and ports allow the sunlight to penetrate to the inside of the leaves to enable the life-giving photosynthesis that is usually carried out by the outside of a plant's leaves or stems.

Not generally considered one of the mimicry-type plants, the genus *Haworthia* has several members that take advantage of the photosynthetic window arrangement. These are not the boldly striped "zebra plants" found in the care of so many grandmothers of the 1950s, but others with thick, fleshy leaves arranged in a traditional rosette pattern with large, flattened translucent leaf tips. These species of *Haworthia* likewise spend their lives buried up to their windows, essentially invisible to the rest of the world.

Lithops, known as living stones or pebble plants, look more like rocks than plants—at least at first glance.

. . . .

(OPPOSITE) Haworthias aren't usually considered one of the classic mimicry succulents, but their fleshy leaves have photosynthetic "windows" at their tips.

Carrion flowers are so named because of their rotting meat stench, which is quite effective at attracting flies.

....

(BELOW & RIGHT) Echeverias are beloved for their beautiful rosette shapes.

Members of the subfamily Asclepiadoideae, which contains succulents as well as many non-succulent plants, use a form of deception. A few of the most popular genera are *Stapelia*, *Carraluma*, *Huernia*, *Orbea*, and *Hoodia*. Collectively known as "carrion flowers," they are perfectly visible, clump-forming plants consisting of upright, highly succulent stems. They are quite varied in appearance from one genus to the next. However, a common thread includes a marvelous, albeit odiferous, tool of deceit: their flowers. Many of them are truly extraterrestrial looking with cool colors. Some sport a shiny lacquered finish and others are barred, striped, spotted, and, yes, even hairy. All of this is topped off with a stench that can only be described as rotting meat or a dead animal—hence the name "carrion

flowers." Their primary pollinators are flies, and nothing draws flies like old roadkill. A prime example is *Stapelia gettleffii*, which, with its background beige-yellow color and narrow darker striping, smell, and very fine, mauve-purple-gray wispy hair, would be a deceased small mammal to any fly!

A Rose Is a Rose Until It's Not

Succulents as a group have many faces, but the overriding design is a symmetrical, multilayered rosette. From the tiniest sedums to massive tree aloes, the water-storing, succulent leaves take on the traditional visage of a garden rose. It is in this group that are found some of the most familiar, trendy, and popular succulents. These plants, which have been around for eons and mostly overlooked except for the occasional wild landscape patch, have become superstars in today's culture. Interior design accents, living wreaths and topiaries, vertical mosaic living walls, container gardens, floral design, and weddings are some of the hottest applications today. These modern-day craft-worthy "roses" include, among others, the genera *Echeveria, Sempervivum, Graptopetalum, Aeonium, Monanthes, Dudleya*, and *Pachyphytum*.

Echeverias are, at this writing, the most sought-after of succulents. They are available in a range of sizes and colors and have been the subject of ongoing hybridization for decades. Species types display a wide palette of pastels along with

some darker and patterned varieties like *E. affinis, E. purpusorum*, and *E. nodulosa*. Texture is not to be ignored either, with *E. pulvinata* and *E. setosa* bringing a fuzzy or hairy note to the mix. One of the most polarizing accents on some echeverias is the caruncle—a knobby, warty, bumpy outcropping of the leaf surface that can be irregular or quite patterned. These were first discovered as an anomaly on a single form of *E. gibbiflora* and formed the foundation of all existing hybrids that have that same trait of carunculated leaves.

Many of the echeverias that form larger rosettes (10 inches (25.4 cm) or more) have also descended from the smoother form of *E. gibbiflora* as cultivars or hybrids of both types. Many of the named varieties of *E. gibbiflora* hybrids available today were created by Dick Wright of Southern California. These are some of the most impressive members of the echeveria group, displaying intricate ruffles, caruncles, and undulated leaves in various colors. Some examples are 'Afterglow', 'Raindrops', 'Arlie Wright', 'Mauna Loa', and 'Cameo'. Two other noted hybridizers, both of Southern California and close colleagues of Dick Wright, are the late Denise Manley, who created the amazing 'Etna', and Renee O'Connell, who is responsible for dozens of today's most sought-after new hybrids. Her creations run the gamut of sizes, colors, and textures, with such beauties as 'Neon Breakers', 'Gorgon's Grotto', 'Blue Frills', and 'Cubic Frost', to name just a few. Other closely related

The fine velvet coat of *Echeveria harmsii* creates a frosty appearance.

. . . .

(OPPOSITE) Called the "painted echeveria" for good reason, *E. nodulosa* is one of the most beautiful species types.

A group of *Echeveria* 'Lola' with mesmerizing natural symmetry.

genera that are part of the echeveria "succulent rose" craze are *Sempervivums*, *Graptopetalum*, *Graptophytum*, *Pachyphytum*, and intergeneric hybrids like *Graptoveria* (*Graptopetalum* × *Echeveria*), *Pachyveria* (*Pachyphytum* × *Echeveria*), and *Sedeveria* (*Sedum* × *Echeveria*).

Opposite of echeverias are Aeoniums with only a few growing single stemmed and at ground level, such as *A. tabulaeforme*. Most have stems or trunks and grow as multiheaded sub-shrubs. Green is the usual color of most aeoniums, with a few renegades like *A. arboreum* 'Atropurpureum', which has varying degrees of purple infusion. *Aeonium* 'Kiwi' is a delightful little multiheaded shrublet sporting small rosettes of green with yellow centers and a red leaf margin.

Hybridizing took the *A. arboreum* 'Atropurpureum' to the well-known 'Zwartkop' with deep purple, near-black leaves. Recent hybrids of acclaim have been introduced by Renee O'Connell, with 'Party Platter' exhibiting the flat rosettes of *A. tabulaeforme* but multibranched like the rest of its parentage. 'Kermit' is another compact, highly branched specimen and 'Mardi Gras' takes *Aeonium* color to new heights with stripes in dark purple, pink, green, red, and yellow!

Creepers, Crawlers, and Hangers

Sedums are some of the most widely spread succulents—some of them are very cold hardy and can be found in locations that regularly freeze and snow. They come

Echeveria harmsii 'Red Velvet' nicely paired with the woolly *Senecio haworthii*.

leaves are eager to start new plants wherever they land.

Ice plants are the floral kings of groundcover and many work well in hanging baskets. Primarily green to gray leafed, they are most known for their unusually large, brightly colored flowers that typically appear in late spring into summer. *Carpobrotus edulis*, often known as pickle weed or hottentot fig, has large, water-filled, long green leaves that are on thick stems capable of growing 3 feet (0.9 m) per year. A single plant can cover an area well over 100 feet (30.5 m) across! More popular genera like *Delosperma* and *Lampranthus* are a bit less aggressive, though still capable of covering an ample amount of ground, and their large flowers are virtually fluorescent in brilliant orange, yellow, purple, pink, and dark red. *Lampranthus deltoides* (previously *Oscularia deltoides*) is fairly cold tolerant with small pink-purple flowers. The plant is remarkable with cherry-red trailing stems and odd delta-shaped, blue-gray leaves akin to plump little pillows. A strikingly beautiful plant is *Senecio mandraliscae*, also known as blue chalk sticks. Unlike the others, the flowers are relatively nondescript, but the long narrow leaves make a true, bright baby-blue statement and stand out wherever planted.

Classic hanging succulents are from completely different genera. The genus *Senecio* gives us *S. rowleyanus*, or string of pearls, with dangling thread-like stems and round leaves not unlike green peas. Less fussy is *S. radicans*, known as string

in all shades of the color spectrum with the exception of black and true blue. Leaf shapes are equally as diverse. A majority have small bead- or bean-shaped leaves, while others have needle-like, round, or oval-shaped leaves. *Sedum* 'Angelina' is particularly attractive, with bright yellow, needle-like leaves in full sun that blush orange under stress. *S. spurium* comes in three color choices of green, the red 'Dragon's Blood', and a variegated 'Tricolor', with leaves swirled in white, pink, and green. Moving into more tender varieties, *S. rubrotinctum* (pork and beans) is a favorite, with shiny green, bean-like leaves tipped in cherry red. It is a popular filler and addition to dish gardens. And like most all other sedums, the easily detached

The forms of sedum species make them great to use as groundcover or as filler in baskets and planters.

of bananas, with long trailing stems covered with plump, crescent, miniature green "bananas." *Ceropegia woodii*, another odd member of the milkweed family, is best known as string of hearts. These succulent dark green leaves are definitely heart-shaped and overlaid with a silver netted pattern. *C. woodii variegata* 'Keepsake Heart', forgoes the dark green and gray for a beautiful random patterning of green, pink, and cream or white. All of these, are well suited as hanging houseplants in a bright location.

(TOP, LEFT) *Delosperma*, like other ice plants, closes in the evening or on a cloudy day.

. . . .

(TOP, RIGHT) String of Pearls (*Senecio rowleyanus*) and other "bead and banana" senecios have a translucent window to aid in photosynthesis.

. . . .

(BOTTOM, RIGHT) A giant among ice plants, *Carpobrotus* will blanket many square yards (meters) of space.

The *Yucca* genus includes nearly forty species.

ASPARAGUS COUSINS

Yuccas, agaves, aloes, and *Manfreda* are landscape plants that, oddly enough, belong to a group related to asparagus. The similarity can be seen in the unopened flower spikes, which look like an oversized version of that favorite vegetable.

Yuccas are both tree-like, such as *Y. elephantipes*, with closer-to-the-ground types like *Y. filamentosa* providing more of a shrub appearance. Usually armed with some sort of leaf tip spine, they are not nearly as dangerous in the landscape as agaves. At maturity, they produce large inflorescences of creamy white flowers.

Agaves are a tremendously varied group in size and color. They can be as small as the 'Confederate Rose' at just 6 to 8 inches (15.2 to 20.3 cm) across, or absolute titans like the century plant, *Agave americana*, with an 8-by-8 foot (2.4-by-2.4 m) body and a flower spike at 30-plus (9.1 m) feet tall! Leaf colors are usually blues and greens, but variegated versions include white-and-yellow striping. *Agave lophantha* 'Quadricolor' stands out as a smaller, more manageable plant suitable for containers as well as the landscape. As the name says, the leaves are a combination of olive green, dark green, and cream that takes on a pink blush during drought and cold. Nearly all agaves are heavily armed with marginal "teeth" and serious terminal spines. The genus *Manfreda* is a colorful agave cousin that is smaller and not armed, and often sports colored patterns, spots, and splotches. Hybrids between the two are becoming more prevalent and are known as *Mangaves*.

Almost everyone knows the medicine plant, *Aloe vera,* but this is just one of a very large family. Similar to agaves as far as their range in size, aloes come as miniatures just a few inches across, like *Aloe* 'Firefly', to towering trees, such as *Aloe barberae,* developing massive trunks and reaching heights of 50 feet (15.2 m) or more. All aloes produce beautiful spikes of flowers primarily in shades of red, orange, pink, and yellow. They are absolute favorites of butterflies and hummingbirds.

Due to their leaves' "teeth" and terminal spines, most *Agave* species (LEFT) warrant caution. While the more colorful *Manfreda* genus (RIGHT) has a similar shape, it doesn't share the same weapons.

Many people know aloe plants from the jelly inside their leaves, which is perhaps most commonly used to soothe burns, but not everyone is familiar with their variety of beautiful shapes and colors. On the left, *Aloe ferox*. Above, A. *barberae*.

....

(OPPOSITE) *Euphorbia trigona* can easily become a large shrub over time in the proper conditions..

Succulent euphorbias have spine-like projections, but their lack of areoles tells us they are not cactuses. Under stress from temperature extremes or drought conditions, aloes perform some of the most impressive color changes.

(LEFT) *Euphorbia trigona* can easily become a large shrub over time in the proper conditions.

EUPHORBIAS: A DIFFERENT STORY

Euphorbias are Old World plants primarily from Africa and Madagascar. They took a course known as convergent evolution—they evolved to fill a niche that imitates the cactuses of the New World. They are not cactuses; they possess a white latex-type sap that can range from mildly irritating to toxic depending on the species and should be avoided as much as possible.

Euphorbias are varied and curious; nearly all are cold tender but able to withstand incredible heat and drought. The shape and size of *Euphorbia obesa*—comparable to a tennis ball—makes it seemingly impossible to be related to the giant candelabra-like trees. In most cases, the flowering parts of a euphorbia are an arrangement of green or yellow bracts but there are species with various hybrids, like *E. milii* (crown of thorns), with larger bracts in red, pink, yellow, white, and spotted "party color" combos. Many of the smaller euphorbias are collector plants because of their odd shapes and subtle patterns and colors. Often, larger euphorbias make better landscape substitutes for cactuses because they look similar and grow faster. The surprise American cousin, one of the very few from the New World, is the poinsettia! This Mexican native is *E. pulcherrima*, and contrary to most accounts, it is one of the least-toxic, least-dangerous euphorbias and doesn't need to be treated as an imminent danger.

❁ Cultural Uses

Many succulents have a long history of cultural applications with some being globally famous and still a part of everyday life.

Agave tequilana
(Tequila Agave/Blue Agave)
Tequila is produced by removing the heart of the plant in its twelfth year. Normally weighing between 80 to 200 pounds (3.6 to 90.7 kg), this heart is stripped of its leaves and pit-roasted to condense and thicken the sap. After, the now honey-like syrup is fermented and distilled. Various types of tequila are enjoyed worldwide. Margarita, anyone?

Aloe species
Aloes of various species have been used for their anesthetic, antibacterial, and tissue-healing properties. Historical uses have included internal consumption for stomach disorders, constipation, insomnia, hemorrhoids, headaches, and mouth and gum disease. The grande dame of all is *Aloe barbadensis* (Aloe vera)—the clear gel inside the leaves of *Aloe vera* has been used as a treatment for internal maladies, insect bites, minor burns, cuts and abrasions, and sunburn, just as it is today.

Euphorbia antisyphilitica (Candelilla)
The stem wax is used for making candles, soaps, and ointments.

Cactuses and
Succulents Outdoors

All plants have some particular claim to fame, and for succulents that is the overwhelming ability to survive in adverse conditions—especially in arid climes or times of drought. The vast majority of succulents come from rainfall-challenged locations that may also be plagued by extreme heat or cold. Coping with temperature extremes is a useful attribute, but the ability to hang on to every last molecule of life-sustaining water can border on miraculous.

In the gardening world, succulents are often lovingly referred to as "fat plants," and their ability to store precious fluids for their survival has made them landscape stars for naturally dry, populated landscapes and areas in the throes of unnatural drought.

There are some plants (usually low-light growers) that are amenable to coming inside and doing quite well, but it's a short list, and for succulents that list is even shorter. Indoor growing, while possible, comes with a litany of challenges to be managed in order to achieve a modicum of success. For this reason, growing succulents outdoors is by far the best-case scenario for healthy, attractive, and colorful succulents.

. . . .

(OPPOSITE) Colorful inflorescences are an added bonus to a well-grown mixed succulent composition.

Succulents are available in a wide range of shapes and sizes to fit your landscape, from tall and tree-like species to low-growing groundcovers.

(TOP) Very old tree aloes (*Aloe dichotoma*) with massive trunks and heavily branched canopies.

....

(BOTTOM) Tree-type euphorbias can serve as "nurse plants," providing protection from the searing sun to the smaller, tenderer plants of the understory.

Cactuses and other succulents may thrive in dry desert conditions, but that doesn't mean they can't suffer from water deficiency. These plants don't need to be watered frequently, but if you notice that they're losing leaves, turning yellow, or collapsing on themselves, it might be time for a good soak.

(TOP, LEFT) Of all the aeoniums, *Aeonium* 'Kiwi' is one of the prettiest and easiest to care for.

(TOP, RIGHT) Black as night, *Aeonium* 'Zwartkop' always stops foot traffic and turns heads.

(LEFT) Color options are endless as well—green is far from the only choice! Above, *Graptopetalum* is the bluish plant on the right; *Aeonium* 'Kiwi' is the pink-and-green plant on the left.

It is very common for many succulents in the harshest, most sun-scorched areas of the world to begin their lives in the proximity of a "nurse plant." This is usually another type of hardy plant under which a young cactus or succulent begins its life and has the blazing sun tempered by an overhead canopy of leaves, stems, or branches. Cactuses may even take advantage of a nonliving "nurse," such as a boulder, small hill, or mound that casts a shadow over the succulent for part of the day. But while this nurse is blocking the sun to some extent, it is only reducing the full-day, full-sun exposure by a fraction. So, planting in an area where the sun is relatively unblocked as it moves through the course of a day is ideal, followed by southern, western, and eastern exposures if dealing with an immovable object like a house, wall, or fence. A northern exposure is the least desirable and will be problematic and not particularly succulent-friendly overall.

Color combinations can be staggering too. Consider pairing the blue of *Senecio mandraliscae* with the near-black of *Aeonium* 'Zwartkop' and the screaming yellow of *Sedum rupestre* 'Angelina'. Often there is an added spectacle in the fall and winter as temperatures begin to dip into the above-freezing but chilly range. Many succulents take on a whole new visage as the temperature stress forces them to adopt blushes of fiery to dark red and brilliant orange tones; many aloes are famous for this. The landscape design is up to the imagination. Look at perhaps using large groupings of boulders to create natural backdrops for the plants as well as provide natural crevices and hollows to plant in. Mimicking a dry streambed is a particularly eye-catching approach that is quite appropriate when designing a landscape composed primarily of cactuses.

Beauty can't be denied when looking at a well-planted succulent landscape, and that beauty comes with lots of bonuses. Succulents are notoriously tough, as is obvious considering their natural habitats. Compared to the typical cottage garden or landscape full of perennials and tropical shrubs and flowers, their care is minimal. They are not heavy feeders, so fertilizing and poor soil are not a major concern. A feeding or two early on in the growing season (the warmer months of the year) using a balanced, all-purpose fertilizer is sufficient.

Watering is often misunderstood when caring for succulents. Because of their ability to survive inhuman aridity and heat, many succulents will go for an enormous length of time without a drop, all the while sacrificing bits of themselves to hang on. They may drop all of their leaves, collapse their stems (or whole bodies, in the case of many cactuses), even disappear completely, retreating to nothing more than a small nub on the surface of the soil that is attached to a still viable swollen root. They look absolutely horrible, if they even "look" at all! When a seasonal rain comes along, these decimated shadows of their former selves fill up like a camel at an oasis and get back to business. This is one reason why the cultivated succulent garden is superior to others. Unlike an English garden, for example, succulents are not going to wilt or fall over if you forgot to water last week, or even a couple of weeks ago. So celebrate the water savings, especially in drought-prone regions and where water costs are high.

Planting large swaths of spreading ice plants on outer perimeters of vacant property leading up to a dwelling, or even hedges of *Crassula ovata* (jade plant), *Portulacaria afra* (elephant bush), or *Opuntia ficus-indica* (beavertail cactus) strategically around buildings, can serve as an excellent firebreak. Being well over 90 percent water in most cases, they starve any fire of usable fuel and squelch an advance to endangered structures. The plants might take a serious beating doing the job, but they usually bounce back after all of the damaged parts are pruned out.

OVERWINTERING FOR COLDER CLIMATES

Regions that are naturally suited for succulent landscapes (along with various deserts) fall under a collective umbrella referred to as a "Mediterranean climate." Succulents from South Africa, Madagascar, Mexico, and the arid locations of Central and South America feel right at home in this relatively perfect, frost-free paradise. The areas of the country that are fortunate enough to have Mediterranean climate conditions are truly spoiled

when it comes to succulent growing outdoors, but areas that receive hard freezing and snow have fewer options for including succulents in their landscape. Most *Sempervivum* spp. thrive through cold periods and aren't afraid of snow or temperatures down to −25°F (−31.7°C). This group is typically found growing in the colder and higher altitudes of Europe and doesn't prefer a Mediterranean climate. There are many sedums that are equally freeze hardy, such as the *Sedum acre*, *S. album*, and *S. reflexum* (down to −25°F [−31.7°C]) and *S. rupestre*, *S. lineare*, and *S. hispanicum* (down to 5°F [−15°C]). There are other succulents, including Yuccas, Agaves, and various cactuses, that are also suitable down to 0°F (−17.8°C), but research is the key. Although this book is not meant to be a cold-hardy succulent reference, the

authors feel it important to let readers know that limited options exist. There are a number of sources dedicated specifically to these types of succulents and their companion plants.

The first step of protection for frost- and freeze-sensitive succulents has to do with water. Water expands when it freezes, so imagine plant cells as tiny water balloons—a water balloon filled to its absolute capacity will easily pop if frozen. If the balloon is only partly filled, it will expand with the freezing water and yet remain intact. The same applies to plant cells. As plants are entering dormancy in late summer or early fall, before the arrival of seasonal frosts or freezes, begin restricting their water. At this stage, the plants either are only slightly growing or have basically stopped altogether. Allowing their cells to partly empty gives them a better chance should a freeze hit.

A freeze or frost is considered "light" if the temperature is just below freezing and for only a few hours in the early morning. Under these conditions, the plants might be completely unfazed or suffer only minor tip burns. Covering plants the night before with a bed sheet, burlap sacks, or horticultural frost cloth (available in most good nursery supply locations) will increase the protection and success. Frost cloth in particular is available in various thicknesses and can offer an extra 4°F to 8°F (–15.6°C to –13.3°C) of protection. The edges of the various covers should be held down on their perimeters with stones or some other type of weight or device. Plastic sheeting is not a good choice as it doesn't allow air circulation, increasing the chance of rotting from trapped moisture and humidity; it can also become a problem when the temperature rises too quickly for the plants to adjust. For extra protection from a longer or colder freeze, a string of Christmas lights laid on the ground, not in touch with the covering ,will help raise the temperature slightly. In the case of taller plants that can handle a light frost but still suffer tip burn, such as frost-tender, columnar cactuses and columnar euphorbias, there is a simple and clever (albeit somewhat silly-looking) solution: Styrofoam cups placed over the tops of each of the columns or branches perform very well in protecting the tender growing tips. This obviously works for shorter plants as well when tip burn is the concern.

These recommendations are helpful in locations where frosts are light and brief and in the case of a rogue frost that's not typical for an area. Keep in mind that locations suffering long, hard, and regular freezes have few, if any, options beyond growing freeze-tolerant plants or moving more tender plants indoors or into greenhouses for the duration.

(OPPOSITE) The toothy *Aloe marlothii* (top) and an *Aloe* hybrid (bottom) frame three favorite jade plants from left to right: *Crassula ovata* 'Gollum', *C. arborescens* (silver dollar plant), and *C. ovata* 'Hummel's Sunset'.

. . . .

(NEXT SPREAD) This collection of color, shape, and texture is like a succulent fiesta.

Aeoniums, crassulas, and senecios make a colorful upright display.

. . . .

(OPPOSITE) A soft, unarmed, monocolored *Agave attenuata* serves as a backdrop for a bright and bold *Aeonium* 'Sunburst'.

For an easy way to check moisture, lay a flat stone on the soil near your plant and check the underside periodically. If there is still moisture under it, it doesn't need water yet.

If soil quality and drainage are concerns in your yard, consider using planters or raised beds. They easily allow you to fine-tune your soil mix. Window box planters are a wonderful no-fuss accent.

SUCCULENT PLANT CARE

Succulents and cactuses are continuing to grow in popularity, as a whole new generation of millennial gardeners is not only captivated by their beguiling beauty but also appreciative of their undemanding care. The survival adaptations of stems, leaves, roots, and trunks that enable the plants to store a life-preserving water supply has contributed to the incredible shapes of these plants. There is an important caveat to succulent culture, however: care often needs to be exacting, without much room for improvisation. Too much water or shade can quickly deteriorate the appearance of many succulents.

Watering Basics

Proper water and ample light are the main contributing factors to the success of succulents either indoors or outdoors. Succulent roots have adapted to optimize the uptake of water when it becomes available. In habitat, this characteristic is vital to a succulent plant's survival. However, in cultivation, this beneficial attribute can have negative consequences. Because succulents are focused on storing water, they do not have the ability to quickly dispose of excess moisture if grown under wet conditions. In combination with cool temperatures, soggy roots begin to succumb to root rot and the plant quickly collapses into a sad, mushy heap. Because the propensity to decompose is always a reality, container succulents should always

be planted in fast-draining soils or commercial cactus mixes.

While the perils of overwatering are real, so too is the pitfall of underwatering. Gardeners often think of the desert as an arid place devoid of all moisture. In reality, many desert plants have root systems that extend into areas many times the diameter of the main plant. So, in times of drought, these spreading root complexes have the ability to use heavy dews or mists. Restricted to a container with smaller root systems, succulents cannot take advantage of these additional sources of moisture. Insufficient water can actually cause the roots to desiccate and die. Succulent growers are responsible for providing the proper amount of water. Usually, the simplest way to water involves drenching the soil and allowing excess water to seep out the drainage hole of the container.

Don't allow plants to sit in saucers of water. Any residual water should be removed. A general rule of thumb is, "If you are not sure whether to water a succulent, don't." Here is a convenient tip that might also help, even with plants in the landscape. Lay a flat stone, like a Mexican beach pebble, on the surface of the soil, near the plant. If there is still moisture under the stone when lifted, do not water. If the area is completely dry, it is time to water again. Remember that most cactuses and other succulents have an active growing period in spring and summer. Once the weather has warmed and other plants are actively growing, it is usually time to begin regular watering.

(TOP, RIGHT) *Graptopetalum* is a fast and furious grower that readily creates crested or "cristate" growths, which can be removed and grown as their own specimen. This massive planting is sporting no fewer than six crests!

(TOP, LEFT) A nearly monochrome green planting becomes interesting when a variety of shapes are the focus

(LEFT) If there is still moisture in the top few inches of soil, your plants can probably go a bit longer before watering.

(OPPOSITE) Bright yellow flower cones are quite the surprise coming out of jet-black aeonium rosettes. Large banks of gray-green *Calandrinia spectabilis* are just beginning to push out tall, graceful stems of deep purple, poppy-like blooms.

One of the biggest benefits to growing succulents outdoors is that you don't have to worry about them getting enough light. However, some species may do better in partial rather than full sun to avoid sunburn.

It's important that whatever kind of soil you use for your succulent, whether you're buying a potting mix or amending the soil in your yard, has good drainage to avoid soggy roots.

Light Requirements

Some growing conditions that would kill other plants don't phase succulents. Intense sunlight combined with extreme heat is a situation that most succulents can endure. Obviously, these settings are not usually found indoors and winter survival often depends on providing as much light as possible. South-facing windows are best for natural sources of light, but supplemental artificial grow lights can be used if such windows are not available.

When grown outdoors, many succulents look their best when protected from the searing rays of the sun. It is extremely important to bear in mind that sunburned leaves can easily occur when moving plants from an indoor location to an outdoor site. In order to prevent burning, plant leaves are covered with a waxy layer called a *cuticle* that thickens when exposed to sunlight, just as a tan protects human skin. Indoors, this cuticle thins out to allow in as much light as possible. Moving a plant directly outdoors can result in permanent scarring, especially on cactuses. Plants can be acclimated to sunnier conditions by putting them in partial shade and then moving gradually to brighter light conditions.

Sufficient light is critical for healthy succulent growth. Poor light can result in etiolated growth, especially on cactuses. Etiolation is a process that occurs with plants grown in insufficient light. It is characterized by long, weak stems; smaller leaves due to longer internodes; and a pale yellow color resulting from a lack of chlorophyll. This is nature's way of increasing the likelihood that a plant will reach a light source, often from under the soil, leaf litter, or shade from competing plants.

Temperature

Although succulents are more cold tolerant than generally assumed, temperature is crucial to their survival. Freezing is a serious problem for many varieties. The ability of plant cells to store water also provides the ideal conditions for those cells to burst under freezing conditions, resulting in the demise of the succulent. Because a desert environment is often characterized by a distinct contrast between nighttime and daytime temperatures, most succulents thrive in colder nights, as long as it remains above freezing. Plants usually prefer daytime temperatures between 70°F and 85°F (21.1°C and 29.4°C) and nighttime temperatures between 50°F and 55°F (10°C and 12.8°C); however, they can survive brief periods well outside of these ranges.

When plants are grown indoors, a drop in temperature can often result in the initiation of flower buds. Locations next to windows often provide the ideal difference in temperature and can satisfy the cooling needed to trigger flowering. Christmas cactuses, *Schlumbergera*, are a good example of this. Many cactuses, especially those that are globe shaped, are far more apt to bloom if given a cool, dry period.

Potting Soils and Planting Mixes

Although light and temperature can be difficult to control, the type of planting medium that succulents are grown in is easier to manage, yet just as essential for healthy plants. Many retailers offer complete, fast-draining potting soils specifically designed for cactuses and succulents. If such a mix is unavailable, an all-purpose soil can be amended with fast-draining products such as perlite and pumice to make it suitable.

Native soils, where most succulents grow, are usually not high in nutrients, so organic material is not as important to their well-being. However, soils rich in microbes are healthier for all plant life. To create a suitable succulent soil medium, use two parts of a non-peat-based potting mix, one part perlite, and one part small-size gravel (like pumice). If gravel is not available, a 1:1 mixture of potting soil and perlite will suffice. It's paramount to create a quick exchange of water and air in the root zone. Soils that stay wet for extended periods will result in the collapse of most succulent plants.

Fertilizer Needs

It is commonly known that succulents need to store water because of the harsh climates in which they grow, but it is less realized that this water-storing ability also allows for the storage of food. For this reason, succulents should be fed sparingly. An excess of food will be stored to the detriment of the plant. It is usually sufficient to feed plants during their growing season with a fertilizer that contains roughly equal proportions of nitrogen, phosphorous, and potassium. Water-soluble foods are best and should be diluted to half the strength that is recommended on the label for other plants.

Day length begins to shorten as fall draws near and the weather begins to cool. This is when succulent plants enter their nonactive rest period. Do not feed plants during this stage of dormancy. There are a few succulents that are winter growers, and they should be fed at this time and allowed to go dormant as spring approaches.

. . . .

(OPPOSITE) This blooming aeonium is backed with a companion drought-tolerant *Salvia leucantha*.

Basics of Succulent Propagation

Collecting and gardening with succulents can quickly turn into a compulsion rivaled only by "orchid fever." But unlike many orchids that can cost hundreds and even thousands of dollars to replicate, a huge number of succulents can be reproduced for pennies. Of course, there are many rare plants that are not cooperative and difficult to reproduce, such as frankincense and *Welwitschia mirabilis* of the Namib Desert. The golf ball cactus, *Mammillaria herrerae*, has been listed as one of nine of the most-threatened plants today. It is classed as critically endangered by the International Union for Conservation of Nature (IUCN). However, it propagates easily from seed and, though threatened in the wild, this cactus has found a permanent home in domestic gardens.

Plant propagators offer hope for the preservation of succulents that are ravaged in the wild by poachers. Fortunately, most of the species that thrive in our homes and gardens are not only easily duplicated, but also fun enough to propagate for the whole family. Here are some of the simplest methods of propagation.

Fine gravel topping holds seeds in place for germination.

Plants that have been propagated by seeds or leaves fill these succulent liner trays.

Seed-grown cactuses ready to be moved to individual pots.

Growing from Seed

Because all cactuses and succulents are flowering plants, they should, in theory, be able to be propagated from seed. Nonetheless, due to the snail's pace growth of some species from seed, other techniques are more practical. Cactus and succulent seeds are available from many online sources, but they can also be collected from plants in the landscape. Fresh seed usually germinates more readily than old seed, so a hands-on approach to seed gathering may produce the best results.

1. It is important to start with clean pots or trays in which to sow the seed. As delicate seedlings germinate, they are especially susceptible to attack from harmful bacteria and fungi. If containers have been used in the past, it is a good idea to disinfect them with a solution of one part bleach to ten parts water. Also, because quick drainage is important, it is often advantageous to use shallow containers that are not deeper than about 4 inches (10.2 cm). Fill them with a planting medium that is equal parts potting soil and either perlite, sharp sand, or pumice. The majority of seeds can germinate in plain sand (not beach sand; it contains too much salt).

Note: Non-metallic planting trays can be sterilized in a microwave. Microwave the soil for about 90 seconds on full power. Allow the soil mix to cool and water it thoroughly. Let it drain, but not dry out completely. If the trays in which the seeds will be planted were not the ones microwaved, fill the propagation pots with the damp soil mixture to about ½ inch (1.3 cm) below the rim.

2. As in nature, most seeds will germinate best if sown in late winter to early spring. Scatter the seeds over loose soil and then press lightly into the mix. Lightly layering the soil with a fine covering of sand to hold the seeds in place is also helpful. Cover the seed trays with clear plastic wrap to hold in moisture and place the trays in a bright location, but out of direct sunlight. Minimum temperatures of 60° to 70°F (15.6°C to 21.1°C) are best for most species, but some tropical species may require warmer conditions (top, right).

3. A significant number of cactuses and succulents will germinate within three weeks, but there are slowpoke species that can require as much as a year to begin growing. Germination times for specific varieties can often be found online. Once seedlings appear, remove the plastic wrap. The soil should not be allowed to dry out, but seedlings are fragile, so when it is time to water, moisten with very fine mists.

4. Once plants are about six months old, they can be transplanted into individual containers. As a general rule, cactuses can be transplanted when they are the size of a large marble and other succulents can be transplanted when they are about 3 inches (7.6 cm) tall. Gently lift the plants from the growing medium in the seed trays, set into the soil of the new container, and water in. Then top-dress the pot with sand, gravel, or pumice, which can help suppress the growth of algae and moss (bottom, right).

Propagation from Stem Cuttings

Propagation by stem cuttings is simple and practical. An unrooted cutting is very easy to establish. The objective is to get it rooted before it dries out too much, because cuttings can actually lose the ability to generate roots once they have become too desiccated. Cuttings taken at the beginning of the growing season will root the quickest. Here are some basic steps to follow.

1. Make the cut. Because pruning shears can crush tissues, it is normally best to use a sharp razor blade or knife that has been sterilized with alcohol to remove a cutting from the parent plant. A clean cut allows the cutting to heal fast enough to survive without water during the callusing stage. Strip leaves from the lower part of the stem (top, left).

2. Dip the cut end in a rooting hormone. This is optional, but many rooting hormones also include an antifungal compound to discourage rot. Many whole-sale growers report success using ground cinnamon as a cheaper alternative to an antifungal treatment. Just sprinkle it onto the cut end (top, right).

3. Let the cutting callus over. During this period, the exposed cut of the succulent is allowed to form a protective callus. This process, which takes about a week to 10 days, is best done in a warm, shady spot outdoors. When a layer of dry, hard tissue has formed over the cut surface, the cutting is ready to plant. The purpose of this dry layer is to dissuade insects and diseases from entering the body of the plant (bottom, left).

4. Prepare the potting mix. As with planting seeds, the mix should be composed of equal parts potting soil and either perlite, sharp sand, or pumice.

5. Select the proper size pot. Containers that allow for a couple of inches of growing should be adequate while the cutting is getting started.

6. Plant the callused stem cutting. Water immediately and then do not water until the soil begins to dry out. Taller cuttings may need to be staked until they root to keep them from falling over. After a few weeks, the succulent stems should have rooted enough to transfer into a larger container. Do not overpot; keep the size of the planter proportionate to the size of the root system (bottom, right).

Multiplication through Leaf Cuttings

Even novice gardeners will find leaf cuttings to be an effortless way of generating countless numbers of new plants. Unlike most leafy plants, a wide range of succulents are very easily propagated in this manner. These are not actual "cuttings," but are carefully removed leaves (with the exception of *Sansevieria*, which are cut leaf segments). Akin to stem cuttings, leaf cuttings are best taken at the beginning of the active growing season. Because of the ease and success rate, this is a great project in which to involve children.

The callusing process is similar to that of stem cuttings as described previously, but usually half the amount of time is required for the leaf end that was attached to the plant to callus over. Once callused, the end of the leaf should just barely be pushed into the soil, as this is where root formation will begin. The small leaves of many sedums are often just scattered over the tops of moistened sand in order to propagate them. Once a new plant has begun to form, the old leaf can be used as a handle to move the baby plant into its new pot.

Some of the groups of succulents that are easily propagated by leaf cuttings include, but are not limited to:

* *Crassula*
* *Echeveria*
* *Gasteria*
* *Graptopetalum*
* *Haworthia*
* *Kalanchoe*
* *Pachyphytum*
* *Sansevieria* (though variegated cultivars may lose their coloring)
* *Sedum*

These succulent stem cuttings with their lower leaves removed are ready for planting. Save the removed leaves—they can be planted too!

Instant Increase with Plantlets and Offsets

A number of cactuses and succulents form offsets, or "babies," that develop around the mother plant. These can be removed and repotted by gently twisting them away from the mother plant. If the offsets are close to the ground, they will have probably already put out a small root system and are ready to be repotted. Numerous succulents, notably sansevierias and agaves, spread by means of underground lateral shoots. As these shoots give rise to new plants, the babies can be severed from the mother plant, callused, and replanted to produce an independent plant.

Some succulents are so teeming with a biological directive to reproduce that it can be a chore just to pick up after them. Included in this group are several *Kalanchoe* spp. that produce small plantlets (often bearing juvenile roots) along the edges of their leaves. These readily detach (they virtually seem to jump from the main plants) and are unbelievably able to create new starter succulents. One *Kalanchoe* plant will be surrounded by dozens or more juvenile plantlets that have fallen from the parent and rooted on their own. *Bryophyllum* is so prolific that its common name is mother-of-thousands!

Agave and furcraea plants grow for many years before finally flowering once and then dying. Small plantlets, called bulbils, form on the old flower stalks and will readily root to become new plants. Once plantlets have been removed from the main plant, they should be treated in a method similar to that discussed for rooting stems. Here is a list of some cactuses and succulent groups that can produce plantlets or offsets:

* *Agave*
* *Aloe*
* *Echinopsis*
* *Furcraea*
* *Kalanchoe*
* *Mammillaria*
* *Sansevieria*

This leaf placed on top of potting soil has begun rooting and forming a plantlet.

. . . .

(OPPOSITE) Leaf and stem cuttings will root and form plantlets without being planted or placed on soil.

3

Cactuses and Succulents Indoors

Succulents don't grow in caves! While this may sound obvious, the attempts homeowners make to bring plants indoors can amount to trying to grow a plant in a deep, dark cavern. Some plants can be acclimated if basic requisites are provided, but for others this is can be mission impossible. Conditions considered creature comforts and necessities to humans often create an alien and oppressive environment for the plant kingdom.

The southern tier of the United States, and other locations globally that fall along the same latitudes, are spoiled with being able to grow a huge array of succulents outdoors with little bother. Further north from there, it becomes even more imperative that indoor culture compensate for extreme seasonal cold—either all year-round or just in the winter months. Staying indoors can save succulents from frosty and freezing conditions, but it can take its toll on their appearance. A general rule of thumb is to grow succulents outdoors for as long as possible during the frost-free months of any climate region. This affords plants maximum time under "normal" conditions to grow and strengthen and be more able to handle the upcoming inside stint. Bring them in before the first seasonal frost hits in fall, and then return them outside after the last danger of frost has passed sometime in spring.

(OPPOSITE) A trio of decorative containers with simple, interesting plantings.

(TOP, LEFT) Spaces between the ranks of leaves showing the stem (internodes) are an indication of stretching or "etiolation." This is a sign of insufficient sunlight, as with this hanging basket sedum.

. . . .

(BOTTOM, LEFT) *Graptosedum* showing some stretching.

. . . .

(TOP, RIGHT) When growing indoors, proper light is key. An enclosed porch with windows on multiple sides is one of the best placement options for keeping your succulents happy and healthy.

. . . .

(BOTTOM, RIGHT) This intergeneric succulent like *Graptoveria* is showing excessive etiolation with widely spaced internodes.

During their winter-protection period, or if they are year-round indoor residents, the following are some things to do for the best possible success.

LET THERE BE LIGHT!

Sufficient light is paramount to raising healthy succulents, and that goes for both outdoor and indoor gardening. Succulents are highly susceptible—they can begin to show the effects after being deprived of proper light conditions for as little as two weeks. This highly disfiguring condition causes severe stretching, blanching and fading of color, and general feeble, weak growth.

Choose a location near an east-, south-, or west-facing window—east and west are the best choices for cactuses and succulents during late spring to fall, and a southern exposure is best during winter when the sun is the lowest in the sky. A northern exposure will always be a bad choice since it generally won't provide sufficient light at any point in the year.

A good supplement, if your space and situation allows, is the use of artificial lighting. There are several options to choose from, but the mainstream reliable choice is fluorescent lighting. Be sure to use bulbs that say "full spectrum"; most of these will have wording in the description that calls out "grow light." Lights need to be suspended no more than 12 inches (30.5 cm) above the plants and be on continuously for at least 12 to 14 hours a day.

There are a few succulent choices that are at home with less light and make great indoor plants. Many haworthias, gasterias, gasteraloes, and sansevierias get along just fine with indirect bright light and no extra angst or fuss. These are some of the most forgiving of the succulents that allow their location in the home to take up residence in places that are really "off limits" to most of the others. This is not something you could do with a *Crassula ovata* (jade plant), as in short order it would begin to stretch and become weak! It is a common desire to take a colorful, mixed succulent planting and display it on a dining room table or an end table in a living room for obvious reasons, but it will not thrive being that far away from a window light source. It is best to move plants into presentation places for guests to view, but move them back once company has left. But, back to our low-light heroes—gasterias and haworthias are happy to take up a spot of honor as a table decoration. Of course, some ambient light is very helpful in preserving the integrity of these plants, for if kept in a dark location, they will begin to show stretching, though it will take a considerably longer time than for other succulents. Consider moving them from time to time to a brighter spot for a chance to enjoy some more perfect conditions that will increase their success when spending time in less-ideal conditions.

Odd numbers of plants plus three completely different shapes and textures turn *Haworthia coarctata* (back), *Adromischus cristata* (right), and *Sempervivum arachnoideum* (left) into an impressive living study in green and white.

Different container materials retain moisture differently, but they all have one thing in common—they need at least one drainage hole in the bottom to make sure excess water can get out.

THE WELL-DRAINING CONTAINER

Beautiful ceramics, plain clay, plastic, and the unconventional solutions—like an old shoe or hollowed pumpkin—all have different effects on watering practices and the retention of moisture in the soil. Whatever your choice, it is imperative that the container have at least one if not several drainage holes in the bottom. Otherwise, all your effort to develop a well-draining soil mix will be for naught: if the water can't get through all of that good, porous soil and exit the container, it will just become a swamp in a pot! Make sure that when you water your succulents they don't end up sitting in saucer water, as this will inevitably end up as a root rot problem. The safest practice is to water all of your plants in a sink or bathtub and return them to their saucers after they have stopped dripping.

Nonporous pots are the best choice if you want to cut down on your plant-related chores, especially if you have a lot of plants. At the same time, porous clay (or even the old boot!) can help avoid the problem of overwatering and accidental soggy soil. In the end, it is all a matter of personal choice as to what works best for the user.

THE IMPORTANCE OF MOISTURE

Indoor succulents are happy with a good thorough drink with a slight drying-out period before repeating during their active growing period, namely what are considered the warmer months of the year, in spring through summer. During these growth months is also the time to feed, if you choose. Winter gets a bit trickier indoors—this is the inactive growth period, so succulents don't want to be taking up vast quantities of water, and definitely not food! What they really want is an occasional watering, just enough to keep the roots plump so they don't collapse. Winter is the time when houses have fireplaces burning or central heating running, which is great for keeping everyone warm and cozy, but any type of potted plant will suffer from the soil being totally sucked dry by the ambient warm and very dry air. This means it is imperative to keep an eye on the soil of your succulents, as it will dry out. If the soil goes bone-dry for too long, it can cause the roots to desiccate to the point of collapse, and then there is little hope of the plant coming back.

And because reduced watering means plants do not get a good flush through the soil in winter like they might in summer, it is a good idea to use purified or distilled water if possible to help avoid the salt buildup that can come from municipal tap water. (Well water is generally not a problem.)

A Handy Moisture Meter Hack: No Batteries Required

Cut a piece of a bamboo skewer, or a cheap, restaurant-style wooden chopstick that is 1 or 2 inches (2.5 or 5 cm) taller than the pot your succulent is in. Insert the stick into the soil all the way to the bottom of the pot and leave in place. Water as you normally do. After a few days, if you want to know whether your succulent needs watering again, just pull out the stick and you will see where the moisture level of the soil is. If it's anywhere between 1 inch (2.5 cm) down from the top of the soil to halfway down the container, that means it's time for another watering. Put the stick back in the pot after checking the moisture level and leave it there until the next time you want to check—it's like a dipstick for your plants!

Tiger jaws (*Faucaria tigrina*) take front stage to some assorted haworthias.

Featured Plants

100 Top Choices of
Cactuses and Succulents

Adenium obesum

DESERT ROSE

FAMILY: Apocynaceae

ORIGIN: Tropical Africa and the Arabian Peninsula

CULTURE: Loves the heat and full sun and needs a very loose, well-drained soil mix. Enjoys regular watering during the warmer months, which are the primary growing period. Actually likes being rootbound. Be careful not to overwater; soil should be allowed to dry out slightly between waterings. Regular fertilizing in spring will promote more abundant flowering. When temperatures begin to dip below 55°F (2.8°C) in the fall, bring containers indoors to a sunny but cool location and reduce watering. Plants are deciduous (lose their leaves) in winter and have a dormant period until spring.

COLD HARDINESS: 40°F (4.4°C)

PROPAGATION: Primarily by seed **BLOOM TIME:** Summer

The desert rose has an interesting swollen base known as a caudex that serves as a water reserve in times of drought. Breeders in Thailand have taken this species and produced a multitude of spectacular hybrids. The trumpet-like flowers can be white, pink, or red, with many new striped hybrids available. Best container grown in most locations because of its sensitivity to cold, plants can be left outdoors in a sunny location during the summer and moved indoors to overwinter. Often grown as a "faux bonsai"; the caudiciform base and plant shape in general are often shown off in a bonsai-type container.

Adromischus cristatus

CRINKLE-LEAF PLANT, KEY LIME PIE

FAMILY: Crassulaceae

ORIGIN: South Africa

CULTURE: Grow in full sun in a well-drained soil and water regularly to occasionally, especially during the growth season from spring to fall.

COLD HARDINESS: 25°F (−3.9°C)

PROPAGATION: By cuttings **BLOOM TIME:** Summer

Succulents take on many shapes reminiscent of the physical world. It may not be too farfetched to imagine the leaves look like a slice of green Key lime pie with a crimped pastry crust.

This is one of the easiest of the *Adromischus* plants to grow. It is low growing, forming very tight clusters that make it an excellent subject for small-container, sunny windowsill culture. Grown almost exclusively for their leaves, it is a spring bloomer with small, green tubular flowers with reddish white flared-out petal tips. These are held on an 8"- (20.3 cm) tall stem above the plant. Flowers are interesting but somewhat inconspicuous.

Aenonium arboreum 'Zwartkop'

BLACK ROSE AENONIUM

FAMILY: Crassulaceae

ORIGIN: Canary Islands

CULTURE: Prefers full sun, coastal and light shade in hottest inland locations. Needs an open, porous soil and regular watering from fall to spring. Reduce water to occasionally in summer and provide some light shade if possible. Protect from frost.

COLD HARDINESS: 30°F (1.1°C)

PROPAGATION: By cuttings   **BLOOM TIME:** Summer

There is disagreement on the correct origin of the name— whether it is the Dutch *Zwartkop* or the German *Schwartzkopf*; however, both mean "black head" and are both generally accepted. This is likely the most recognizable of all the aeonium cultivars and hybrids, with its incredibly dark purple to near-black, rubbery leaves. Unlike most other succulents, black rose is a winter-growing species that is semi-dormant in summer and early fall when foliage is at its darkest. The summer bloom is an amazing large, cone-shaped inflorescence of thousands of small yellow, star-shaped flowers. Like many aeoniums, 'Zwartkop' is monocarpic, meaning that the stem that is blooming will die when the flowers are done. Lower, non-blooming stems typically carry on blooming the following year. The bottom right photo shows an interesting unknown *A. arboretum* hybrid or cultivar.

Aeonium haworthii Hybrid
'KIWI'

FAMILY: Crassulaceae

ORIGIN: Canary Islands

CULTURE: Prefers full sun, coastal and light shade in hottest inland locations. Needs an open, porous soil and regular watering from fall to spring. Reduce water to occasionally in summer and provide some light shade if possible; slight cold hardiness but best to protect from frost.

COLD HARDINESS: 25° to 30°F (−3.9 to −1.1°C)

PROPAGATION: By cuttings

BLOOM TIME: Spring

Always popular, this is one of the easiest and most attractive of the aeoniums. It is a highly branching, sub-shrub-type plant with highly colorful rosettes of lime green and yellow with crimson-red leaf margins. It can readily grow 2' to 3' (0.6 to 0.9 m) tall and about 2' (0.6 m) wide over time. When planted in combination with the darker aeoniums, like 'Zwartkop', it creates a breathtaking visual contrast. The actual name and identity of this aeonium is somewhat murky and still contested. It can be found as *A. percarneum* 'Kiwi' as well as *A. haworthii* 'Tricolor'. The frequently used *A. haworthii* hybrid is equally undefined regarding whether it is a natural or man-made hybrid. Needs full sun, well-draining soil, and regular to occasional watering, it does have a fair hardiness to cold but is best protected from any extended hard frost.

Aeonium Hybrid
'MARDI GRAS'

FAMILY: Crassulaceae

ORIGIN: Nursery-grown hybrid

CULTURE: Prefers full sun in coastal locations, and light shade in the hottest inland locations. Needs an open, porous soil and regular watering from fall to spring. For best color, regular monthly feeding from fall to spring is recommended. Water only occasionally in summer and provide some light shade if possible. Best to protect it from frost.

COLD HARDINESS: 30° to 32°F (−1.1 to 0°C)

PROPAGATION: By cuttings

BLOOM TIME: Spring

This outstanding hybrid was created by Renee O'Connell of San Diego, California, after years of complex crossbreeding. The resulting plant is compact and early branching with kaleidoscopic rosettes. The leaves are a satiny yellow with apple-green mid-stripes. Further highlighting these colors are rose-painted margins that in cooler weather become a rich, dark burgundy. While most aeoniums are not heavy feeders, 'Mardi Gras' is at its best and most reliable color with regular monthly feeding with a diluted fertilizer during its active growth period of fall to spring. With aeoniums generally being monocarpic and dying after the main head flowers, the multiple branching helps to mitigate this problem. Like most others, it is summer dormant. The bulk of species aeoniums originate in the Canary Islands.

Agave

'CONFEDERATE ROSE'

FAMILY: Asparagaceae

ORIGIN: Mexico

CULTURE: Best performance is in full sun with well-draining soil. Responds well to watering during the spring through summer active growth period. Needs infrequent watering once established but looks better with supplemental watering in the hottest of months. Watering should be reduced in winter, and it should be protected from hard frosts.

COLD HARDINESS: 30°F (–1.1°C)

PROPAGATION: By offsets

BLOOM TIME: Infrequently, at maturity

This is a terrific small century plant that is anything but shy when it comes to making offsets, or "pups." It is highly prolific, forming dense clumps or colonies in a fairly short amount of time. These compact, very blue-gray rosettes rarely reach 12" wide, making them a favorite container agave. As attractive as they are, they are heavily armed with marginal teeth and a vicious terminal spine. No species name is called out on this plant, as the actual species is the subject of a lengthy and, as yet, undetermined debate. It had been thought to be a cultivar of *A. parrasana*; however, most recent opinions are leaning to it being a cultivar of *A. potatorum*.

Agave Hybrid

'BLUE GLOW'

FAMILY: Asparagaceae

ORIGIN: Mexico

CULTURE: Best performance is in full sun with well-draining soil. Responds well to watering during the spring through summer active growth period. Needs infrequent watering once established but looks better with supplemental watering in the hottest of months. Watering should be reduced in winter.

COLD HARDINESS: 25°F (–3.9°C), possibly lower

PROPAGATION: By offsets

BLOOM TIME: Infrequently, at maturity

A relatively new hybrid from breeder Kelly Griffin of San Diego, this plant is a result of the combination of *A. attenuata* crossed with *A. ocahui*. Unlike most hybrids, this one curiously does not really resemble either parent in any overtly obvious way. Blue-green leaves less than 2"(5.1 cm) wide have red margins edged with yellow and bear tiny soft spines. Each leaf is tipped with a short red spine. The namesake 'Blue Glow' is most expressed with any type of backlighting from the sun. The red and yellow leaf margins truly "glow" in this exposure. This is more of a medium-size century plant about 2' tall by 3' wide (0.6 m tall by 0.9 m wide). This plant should not be confused with the hybrid 'Blue Flame', which is a much larger plant.

Agave lophantha 'Quadricolor'
QUADRICOLOR CENTURY PLANT

FAMILY: Asparagaceae

ORIGIN: Mexico

CULTURE: Best performance is in full sun with well-draining soil. Responds well to watering during the spring through summer active growth period. Needs infrequent watering once established but looks better with supplemental watering in the hottest of months. Watering should be reduced in winter.

COLD HARDINESS: 15°F (–9.4°C)

PROPAGATION: By offsets

BLOOM TIME: Infrequently, at maturity

Here is an amazingly beautiful, smaller agave that is not only a stunner in the landscape but also perfectly suited to container growing. Only reaching 1' to 2' (0.3 m to 0.6 m) tall and wide, it is a riot of color. Each leaf has wide yellow margins with a dark green midsection that is split down the center with a light green stripe. The very edge of the leaf is armed with small, red-brown teeth that become redder in times of stress, such as extreme heat, cold, or drought. *Agave lophantha* 'Quadricolor' makes a dazzling specimen either in a container or in the ground from Zone 8 south.

Agave victoriae-reginae
QUEEN VICTORIA AGAVE

FAMILY: Asparagaceae

ORIGIN: Mexico

CULTURE: Best performance is in full sun or light shade with well-draining soil. Responds well to watering during the spring through summer active growth period. Needs infrequent watering once established but looks better with supplemental watering in the hottest of months. Watering should be reduced in winter.

COLD HARDINESS: 15°F (–9.4°C)

PROPAGATION: By offsets, seed

BLOOM TIME: Infrequently, at maturity

Less than 1' (0.3 m) tall and less than 2' (0.6 m) wide, this is one of the most attractive Agaves in existence, with an outstanding symmetry displayed by its densely packed leaves. Very thick geometric leaves, with a noticeable keel, are marked with pure white margins and repetitive white-lined patterns on the keel side. This is a favorite visual ornamental. Should it flower, which usually is after many years, it puts forth, for a fairly small plant, a very tall, unbranched spike that can reach to 15' (4.6 m) tall! It has densely packed reddish purple flowers. After flowering, unless it has previously put out some offsets, the blooming plant will have to be replaced. There are also other uniquely beautiful variegated forms, such as 'Golden Princess' and 'White Rhino'.

Alluaudia procera

MADAGASCAN OCOTILLO, FALSE OCOTILLO

FAMILY: Didiereaceae

ORIGIN: Madagascar

CULTURE: Best performance is in full sun or light shade with well-draining soil. Responds well to watering during the spring through summer active growth period. Needs infrequent watering once established but looks better with supplemental watering in the hottest of months. Watering should be reduced in winter.

COLD HARDINESS: 25°F (–3.9°C)

PROPAGATION: By cuttings

BLOOM TIME: Infrequently

Like nearly everything else in Madagascar, this is a fascinating, unusual plant. Occasionally branching, this is typically an upright, unbranched plant that can grow 15' to 25' (4.6 to 7.6 m) tall in nature but is usually shorter in cultivation. In its native habitat in the spiny forests of southwestern Madagascar, there are reports that the plant can reach to 60' tall. The typical trunk or stem diameter is 1" to 2" (2.5 to 5.1 cm), with the base becoming much larger over time to support the upright growth. The stems are covered top to bottom with rows of spines, and after the rainy season, a pair of small oval leaves sprout below each spine. The most interesting part is the leaf orientation. After losing all leaves to conserve moisture and water loss after the seasonal rains have gone, the plants remain leafless and semi-dormant until the next rains. When the rains return, any new length of the stem that was added from the previous growing season sprouts leaves that are horizontal to the ground to stop and catch as many raindrops as possible. All other leaves down the entire length of the plant emerge vertically to direct the rainwater from the top straight down to the root zone. In the following season, those leaves that were horizontal become vertical, with new horizontal leaves above them!

Aloe barbadensis

MEDICINE PLANT, ALOE VERA

FAMILY: Asphodelaceae

ORIGIN: North Africa, Arabian Peninsula

CULTURE: Grow in full sun to light shade with porous, well-draining soil. Water regularly to occasionally spring to fall, allowing the soil to dry before watering again. Keep on the dry side in winter, watering only occasionally, and protect from frost.

COLD HARDINESS: 35°F (1.7°C)

PROPAGATION: By seed, offsets

BLOOM TIME: Summer

Very few succulents—in fact, possibly no other succulents—are as well known as *Aloe barbadensis*, more commonly known as aloe vera. The health and medicinal properties of this plant are known and used globally. They include burn treatment, lowering blood sugar, natural laxative, and heartburn relief. Because of this, it is found growing well outside of its native habitat in tropical areas everywhere. Grown as a houseplant, it needs an extremely sunny, bright location to remain healthy. Grown outdoors where possible, plants can reach 2' (0.6 m) tall and in full sun take on a light coppery-bronze color. Flowers appear on a spike held above the plant and are yellow and tubular, much to the delight of hummingbirds.

Aloe barberae

GIANT TREE ALOE

FAMILY: Asphodelaceae

ORIGIN: South Africa

CULTURE: Plant in full sun or light shade in a fairly well-drained soil and water only occasionally to infrequently once established. Water little to none in the winter.

COLD HARDINESS: 25°F (–3.9°C)

PROPAGATION: By seed, cuttings

BLOOM TIME: Fall to winter

The largest, grandest of the tree-like aloes, *A. barberae* makes an impactful architectural statement where it can be grown outdoors. This is a relatively fast-growing tree that develops a thick buttressed base to support the weight of the wide canopy. Branching nearly always occurs at the point where a previous bloom spike has appeared, thus constantly creating more and more potentially blooming branches. An impressive canopy is quickly created. The flowers are an attractive peach color on an inflorescence about 1' (0.3 m) long. This is not a messy plant, which makes it a favorite for use by pools and walkways. It actually grows quite well for a long time in a large container. There are a few exceptional hybrids of this species now available in cultivation: *Aloe* 'Goliath' (*A. barberae* × *A. vaombe*) and *Aloe* 'Hercules' (*A. barberae* × *A. dichotoma*). These are attractive plants with a shorter, more compact habit. *Aloe barberae* is often still found listed by the previous name of *Aloe bainesii*.

Aloe Hybrid
'BLIZZARD'

FAMILY: Asphodelaceae   **ORIGIN:** Nursery hybrid

CULTURE: Needs full sun to light shade with an open, well-draining soil. Water thoroughly during warmer months and allow soil to dry before watering again. Reduce watering in winter and protect from frost.

COLD HARDINESS: 28°F (–2.2°C)

PROPAGATION: By offsets   **BLOOM TIME:** Fall to winter

Attention-getting and cute as a button, this is one blizzard that gardeners can welcome. This striking little aloe hybrid was created by Renee O'Connell of San Diego using *Aloe* 'Doran Black' and another proprietary hybrid of her creation. Perfect for container growing and indoor culture with sufficient light, this has a very compact, upright habit. The foliage is barred with snow white and narrower dark green bands. Plants should be protected from afternoon sun in hot climates. It not only blooms in fall and winter but off and on through the year as well. The flowers are an orange, coral-apricot color. It freely produces offsets.

Aloe Hybrid
'FIREBIRD'

FAMILY: Asphodelaceae   **ORIGIN:** Nursery hybrid

CULTURE: Needs full sun to light shade with an open, well-draining soil. Water thoroughly during warmer months and allow soil to dry before watering again. Reduce watering in winter and protect from frost.

COLD HARDINESS: 28°F (–2.2°C)

PROPAGATION: By offsets   **BLOOM TIME:** Frequent, anytime

This is a blooming powerhouse and only 6" to 7" (15.2 to 17.8 cm) across with slender leaves and a loose habit. The olive-green leaves are only slightly dappled with light green to white dots and dashes. The flower stems hold small, extremely attractive, very bright tangerine flowers—their color is not a typical aloe pinky-orange. This hybrid was created by Shannon Lyons in the 1980s using *A. descoingsii* and *A. thompsoniae*. A superb choice for attracting hummingbirds.

Aloe Hybrid

'OIK'

FAMILY: Asphodelaceae **ORIGIN:** Nursery hybrid

CULTURE: Needs full sun to light shade with an open, well-draining soil. Water thoroughly during warmer months and allow soil to dry before watering again. Reduce watering in winter and protect from frost.

COLD HARDINESS: 28°F (−2.2°C)

PROPAGATION: By offsets **BLOOM TIME:** Fall to winter

Depending on the time of year and the amount of external stress from heat, cold, or drought, the short triangular leaves will favor either more of a blue or a green background color. In amazing contrast, the leaf surfaces are covered with raised singular or merged dark pink teeth appearing as raised, pointed dots and dashes. Teeth of the same dark pink color line the leaf margins. These are narrow and square to rectangular in various lengths, looking very reminiscent of the blade on a chainsaw—very unique. This is one of several hybrids created by Karen Zimmerman. The word *oik*, in its mildest sense, is British slang for a rowdy or unruly child.

Aloe juvenna

TIGER TOOTH ALOE

FAMILY: Asphodelaceae **ORIGIN:** Kenya

CULTURE: Grow in full sun to light shade with porous, well-draining soil. Water regularly to occasionally spring to fall (will appreciate more during the hottest months), allowing the soil to dry slightly before watering again. Keep on the dry side in winter, watering only occasionally, and protect from a hard frost.

COLD HARDINESS: 25°F (−3.9°C)

PROPAGATION: By cuttings **BLOOM TIME:** Infrequently

Aloe juvenna is a small, clump-forming succulent. The leaves are speckled with light green and white irregular spots, and the margins are armed with light green to yellow showy teeth. In times of extreme heat, drought, or cold, the plant takes on a pleasant red blush. This aloe creates a dense colony that is suitable for both dry garden planting and containers. While the orange-red, small tubular flowers are appreciated by hummingbirds, they appear infrequently. Tiger tooth aloe is quite often found incorrectly labeled as *Aloe zanzibarica*.

Aloe plicatilis

FAN ALOE

FAMILY: Asphodelaceae

ORIGIN: South Africa

CULTURE: Needs full sun in most locations, with light shade in hotter inland areas. Soil should be well draining; water occasionally during summer months. Reduce watering in the winter.

COLD HARDINESS: 25°F (–3.9°C)

PROPAGATION: By seed, cuttings

BLOOM TIME: Winter to spring

Primarily shrub-like and growing 4' to 8' (1.2 to 2.4 m) tall and approximately 6' (1.8 m) wide in regular cultivation, *Aloe plicatilis* can be taller and more tree-like in its native habitat. The habit is multiple branching, with each branch being topped with ranks of oppositely stacked leaves resembling 1'- (0.3 m) long, gray-green curved tongue depressors. Leaves with single plane symmetry give the appearance of a flat, folding fan. The trunk has corky, fire-resistant bark and the branches fork into pairs without a central leader, a pattern known as "dichotomous" branching. Each terminal leaf cluster will eventually bear a 1' to 2' (0.3 m to 0.6 m) flower spike supporting dozens of pink tubular flowers—a favorite of hummingbirds in the United States and sunbirds in its native habitat.

Aloe variegata

PARTRIDGE BREAST ALOE, TIGER ALOE

FAMILY: Asphodelaceae

ORIGIN: South Africa

CULTURE: Cool sun to light shade exposure with very well-draining soil. Little to occasional watering.

COLD HARDINESS: 20°–25°F

PROPAGATION: By seed, offsets

BLOOM TIME: Winter

Requiring less light than most other species in the genus, this unusual and beautiful aloe is one of the few that works well as a houseplant. A smaller aloe, it grows about 10 to 12" (25.4 to 30.5 cm) tall to 9" (22.9 cm) wide and forms rosettes with leaves arranged in three ranks that are upright with a boat-hull shape and a distinct indentation down the middle. *Aloe variegata* is so hardy that it can survive for several seasons with no water in the wild, although the leaves take on a reddish tinge and the plant won't look happy. The common names come from the silvery speckles on the leaves. The tubular, nectar-laden coral flowers are held on a spike above the plant and are a favorite of hummingbirds.

Anacampseros telephiastrum variegata
'SUNRISE'

FAMILY: Portulacaceae

ORIGIN: South Africa

CULTURE: Does best in very bright light or filtered, dappled sun. Needs porous, well-draining soil and regular watering in the warmest months; allow the soil to dry slightly before watering again. Reduce watering in winter and protect from frost.

COLD HARDINESS: 35°F (1.7°C)

PROPAGATION: By cuttings

BLOOM TIME: Summer

Naturally, the form of this plant is rather drab in dark olive green with dark purple undersides, which helps it remain camouflaged against its native gravelly substrate to avoid being eaten by local wildlife seeking moisture. This beautiful form must come to market as a sport from a cultivated plant, as it would not survive predation in the wild. The small rosettes are almost jewel-like, glowing with intense rose, lime, and emerald green, with violet pink on the undersides of the leaves. In summer, 2" to 3" (5.1 to 7.6 cm) stems arise and support single or multiple buds, which become beautiful, relatively large pink flowers that are open for only a few hours in the afternoon. The plant's rosettes are very tight and compact, but slowly and eventually take on a trailing habit with age.

Astrophytum myriostigma
BISHOP'S CAP CACTUS

FAMILY: Cactaceae

ORIGIN: Northern and central Mexico

CULTURE: Grow in full sun to light shade with porous, very well-draining soil. Water sparingly from March until October and keep perfectly dry in winter.

COLD HARDINESS: 20° to 25°F (–6.7 to –3.9°C)

PROPAGATION: By seed only

BLOOM TIME: Intermittent spring through summer

This is a relatively slow-growing genus of cactuses usually seen as small plants; however, they can reach 2' to 3' (0.6 m to 0.9 m) tall over time, but they require a lot of patience to reach their full potential. Gray-white bodies of these cactuses have adapted to be colored much like the limestone sub- strate they grow on so that the plants are nearly invisible to potential predators. In bloom, it is topped with glossy yellow, sweet-scented flowers. Keep the soil dry as soon as temperatures start dropping in October, as it tends to rot at that time of year if kept wet. The thornless nature of this plant makes it a favorite of "spine shy" hobbyists. *A. myriostigma* has been the subject of passionate breeding and selection by the Japanese. The plant first arrived in Japan in 1868, just 30 years after its discovery, and the cultivars that have been grown are alien enough for the most obsessed collectors of oddities.

Bowiea volubilis

CLIMBING ONION, SEA ONION

FAMILY: Asparagaceae **ORIGIN:** South Africa

CULTURE: Needs porous, well-draining soil and prefers full to part sun. Water regularly during growth period, winter to spring, allowing soil to dry out in betweeen. The plant is dormant in summer, so water little to none. Protect from frost.

COLD HARDINESS: 40°F (4.4°C)

PROPAGATION: By division **BLOOM TIME:** Winter to spring

In its native habitat, the climbing onion is often covered in the local substrate, but it is much more interesting in cultivation with the bulb exposed above the soil. In late winter, the bulb develops a new, branched, scrambling or twining green flowering stem. Support is helpful, as this vine can top 6' (1.8 m) in length. Small star-shaped green flowers with an unpleasant aroma appear after the vine has extended. Once the plant has finished its growth it will go into dormancy, which is usually in the summer. At this time the vine will begin to dry, and the entire stem should be cut off at the bulb.

Cephalocereus senilis

OLD MAN CACTUS, OLD MAN OF MEXICO

FAMILY: Cactaceae **ORIGIN:** Mexico

CULTURE: Needs very porous, well-draining soil and full to partial sun. Provide little to moderate water from spring to summer, and almost none in winter.

COLD HARDINESS: 20°F (–6.7°C)

PROPAGATION: By seed **BLOOM TIME:** Spring

Googly eyes are often added to this plant as a novelty. One look at it captures the imagination of every cactophile. It is one of the most famous and recognized of the "Old Men" cactuses. It is extremely slow growing and in nature can take up to 20 years to reach 2' (0.6 m) tall. In cultivation, this is sped up somewhat with more consistent care. The long "hair" is a modification of the radial spines that give the plant extra protection from the sun, cold, or frost. The central spine is still present and quite a formidable defense. Taking at least 10 years to reach blooming maturity, flowers are rarely seen in cultivation.

Cereus peruvianus/C. repandus
PERUVIAN APPLE CACTUS

FAMILY: Cactaceae **ORIGIN:** South America

CULTURE: Needs porous, well-draining soil and regular watering during the warmer months; reduce watering in winter.

COLD HARDINESS: 28°F (–2.2°C)

PROPAGATION: By seed, cuttings **BLOOM TIME:** Spring to summer

Peruvian apples make a useful landscape plant for frost-free locations or those with short, light frost events. It is fast growing, often 2' (0.6 m) or more per year, and becomes quite wide, branched, and tree-like. It enjoys more regular watering than most cactuses and produces very large, white, fragrant flowers. The added bonus of this cactus is the large, spineless, and delicious fruit! Like dragon fruit (*Hylocereus* spp.) but smaller, the round fruits ripen to a beautiful red color and are filled with a sweet white flesh flecked with tiny black, crunchy, edible seeds. The native name for the fruit in Latin America is *pitaya*.

Ceropegia sandersonii
PARACHUTE PLANT, UMBRELLA PLANT

FAMILY: Apocynaceae **ORIGIN:** Mozambique, South Africa

CULTURE: Needs full to part sun; porous, well-draining soil; and regular watering during the growth period (spring and summer), allowing soil to dry slightly before watering again. Reduce watering in winter and protect from frost.

COLD HARDINESS: 35°F (1.7°C)

PROPAGATION: By cuttings, seed **BLOOM TIME:** Summer

Members of the *Ceropegia* genus are nature's oddities. A trailing, vining plant, it has heart-shaped leaves and alien-looking flowers. Green with darker speckles and a slightly hairy margin, the petals remain attached at their tips, forming a tented tube with five openings around the perimeter. Simulating the scent of an injured bee, the flowers lure flies into the openings, which crawl down into the funnel-like tube, finding themselves covered in pollen and trapped by numerous downward-facing hairs. The flies remain there until the flower begins to end its bloom cycle and the hairs become too weak to resist their escape. They then crawl out and proceed to repeat the process, thus pollinating other flowers—a benevolent fly trap compared to some others.

Ceropegia woodii

STRING OF HEARTS, ROSARY VINE

FAMILY: Apocynaceae

ORIGIN: South Africa, Swaziland, Zimbabwe

CULTURE: Needs part sun to light shade; porous, well-draining soil; and regular watering during the growth period (spring to summer), allowing soil to dry before watering again. Reduce watering in winter and protect from frost.

COLD HARDINESS: 50°F (10°C)

PROPAGATION: By cuttings, seed

BLOOM TIME: Summer

Another unusual tropical *Ceropegia* is a favorite houseplant that thrives in normal household temperatures with positioning in brightly lit locations. The dark green, heart-shaped leaves are decorated by a silvery, lace-like overlay and dark purple undersides. Not shy about blooming, the oddly shaped, tubular flowers are more or less a flamingo-pink with five stringy, near black, furry petals that are joined at their tips, forming a small cage-like structure. This is traditionally grown as a hanging plant and can become quite long over time. The variety 'Variegata', known as keepsake hearts, has leaves with a beautiful wide ivory or cream margin, a dark green center, and pink undersides.

Consolea rubescens

ROAD KILL CACTUS

FAMILY: Cactaceae

ORIGIN: West Indies, Caribbean

CULTURE: Grow in full sun with porous, well-draining soil. Water regularly spring to fall, allowing soil to dry between applications. Keep on the dry side in winter, watering only occasionally, and protect from frost.

COLD HARDINESS: 35°F (1.7°C)

PROPAGATION: By cuttings

BLOOM TIME: Summer

This plant was previously known as *Opuntia rubescens*, and there is still discussion as to its actual classification. This is one of the tree-like, or "arborescent," cactuses that can grow in excess of 15' (4.6 m) tall. When younger, this is truly one of the more unusual and comical cactuses, with extremely flattened pads. The whole plant looks as if it had been hit by a car, hence the common name "road kill cactus." When looked at side-on, it almost becomes invisible, like a cardboard cutout viewed on edge. As it matures, the trunk puts on a fair girth of 6" (15.2 cm) or more in diameter, taking on an oval to round shape. Branching with age, it still sports the long, flattened oval pads. These are evenly dotted with raised areoles that have very short, nearly unnoticeable spines, making it more "user friendly" than most. In summer, the pads put forth numerous yellow to orange flowers followed by small fruits. Being a Caribbean native, it is more receptive to regular watering but also more frost tender.

Cotyledon orbiculata var. *oblonga* 'Undulata'
SILVER RUFFLES

FAMILY: Crassulaceae

ORIGIN: South Africa

CULTURE: Well-draining porous soil, water only occasionally, full sun for best appearance.

COLD HARDINESS: 25° to 30°F (–3.9 to –1.1°C)

PROPAGATION: By cuttings

BLOOM TIME: Summer

One of the little treasures of life, this attractive sub-shrub is only slightly branching and grows 18" to 24"(45.7 to 61 cm) tall. The leaves have a very tightly undulated edge not unlike the side of a lasagna noodle, and they are coated with a very silvery-white, waxy bloom. Take care not to water from above, as this will remove the attractive coating. To add to the beauty, summertime brings forth roughly 12"(30.5 cm)–tall flower spikes with numerous pendent, bell-like, red-orange flowers that are frequented by local hummingbirds.

Crassula perfoliate var. *falcata*
PROPELLER PLANT

FAMILY: Crassulaceae

ORIGIN: South Africa

CULTURE: Needs porous, well-draining soil and tolerates regular watering during all warmer months; reduce water in winter. Place in full sun to light shade, and protect from frost.

COLD HARDINESS: 35°F (1.7°C)

PROPAGATION: By cuttings

BLOOM TIME: Summer

The thick, gray-green sickle-shaped leaves form tightly grouped stacking pairs, adding a fan effect to the overall appearance. In summer, flower spikes appear carrying large heads of small orange-red to scarlet-red fragrant flowers that remain for up to a month. They have a very heavy, floral aroma that on a summer day can be smelled from quite a distance. Up close, a whiff is intoxicating but quickly becomes too strong to handle and is best enjoyed from farther away.

Crassula ovata

JADE PLANT, GOOD LUCK JADE

FAMILY: Crassulaceae

ORIGIN: South Africa, Mozambique

CULTURE: Needs porous, well-draining soil that should be allowed to dry out well before watering again. Full sun is needed for best growth and flowering; protect from hard frost.

COLD HARDINESS: 28°F (–2.2°C)

PROPAGATION: By cuttings

BLOOM TIME: Winter

One of the most popular houseplants, jade plant has rich green, succulent leaves considered by some to represent money, wealth, and prosperity. Indoors, jade plants need as much full sun to bright light as possible. Lack of sufficient light will cause the plant to stretch and become stringy and weak. When watering, do it thoroughly and do not water again until the soil has become almost completely dry—and never let it sit in standing water for any length of time. In the ground in full sun and light-frost or frost-free locations, the leaves often have a bright red margin, and it produces clusters of small, star-shaped, white flowers in winter that nearly cover the plant. These plants can easily become 6' (1.8 m) hedges. Plants grown indoors rarely if ever flower due to lack of constant full sun. There are many varieties and cultivars as well, such as the variegated 'Hummel's Sunset' and the pink-flowered 'Pacific Pink'.

Crassula ovata
'GOLLUM' JADE

FAMILY: Crassulaceae

ORIGIN: South Africa, Mozambique

CULTURE: Needs porous, well-draining soil that should be allowed to dry out well before watering again. Full sun is needed for best growth and flowering; protect from hard frost.

COLD HARDINESS: 28°F (2.2°C)

PROPAGATION: By cuttings

BLOOM TIME: Winter

'Gollum' is one of several fun, monstrose-type sports or cultivars of the traditional jade. Care and culture are the same as for the regular *Crassula ovata*, the only difference being the appearance. The leaves are mutated to be basically rolled over into a cylindrical shape with a suction cup–like dimple at the end. The plant is slower growing and planted in the ground outside where conditions allow, and the overall size is significantly smaller. Other fun forms with similar but differently shaped leaves are 'Hobbit', 'Ogre Ears', and 'E.T.'s Fingers'. Some of these can also be found in variegated versions. Along with the traditional jade plant, these varieties all lend themselves to pruning and sculpting into quite attractive succulent bonsai subjects.

Cyphostemma juttae

WILD GRAPE, TREE GRAPE

FAMILY: Vitaceae

ORIGIN: Southern Africa

CULTURE: Needs very well-draining soil and full to part sun. Water only when in leaf, usually in late spring to summer.

COLD HARDINESS: 25° to 30°F (–3.9 to –1.1°C)

PROPAGATION: By seed

BLOOM TIME: Summer

Cyphostemma is a much-desired plant for the garden, as are other caudiciform plants. They make superb container or open garden additions, especially around swimming pools and in courtyards. This amazing caudiciform relative of the common grape is known for its large swollen base (caudex). As it leafs out in summer, clusters of tiny insignificant flowers are produced, which proceed to develop grape-like fruits that turn red when ripe. Though related to table grapes, this fruit is inedible and contains various chemical toxins. Reaching tree-like proportions in the wild, cultivated plants are usually 2' to 4' (0.6 m to 1.2 m) tall on average. Tree grapes are native to Namibia, where they are exposed to very dry and hot conditions. The large caudex becomes a backup reservoir of water to survive extended periods of drought. In winter, the plant becomes deciduous and drops all its leaves and remains so until spring or early summer.

Dudleya brittonii

GIANT CHALK DUDLEYA

FAMILY: Crassulaceae

ORIGIN: Baja California, Mexico

CULTURE: Must have very porous, well-draining soil and full sun. Water from fall to spring with only the slightest irrigation in summer.

COLD HARDINESS: 15°F (−9.4°C)

PROPAGATION: By cuttings, seed

BLOOM TIME: Spring to summer

No gardener is ever ambivalent at the first sight of this brilliantly chalky-white Baja California, Mexico–native succulent. This Dudleya is known for its huge (up to 18" [46 cm] wide) chalky-white rosettes that seem to have a ghostly glow. Mostly solitary but occasionally putting out offsets, it is found growing on hillsides and out of rocky cliff crevices. Silvery-white 2' (0.6 m)-tall flower spikes appear in spring and change color to a dark cherry red while sporting clusters of yellow flowers. Their cliffside habit makes them perfect for planting in cracks and crevices in rock walls and rock gardens. Summer watering should be just the very bare minimum, and try to avoid overhead watering at this time.

Echeveria Hybrid
'BLACK PRINCE'

FAMILY: Crassulaceae

ORIGIN: Nursery hybrid

CULTURE: Needs porous, well-draining soil with full sun to light shade in the hottest inland locations. Water thoroughly and allow the soil to dry out some before thoroughly watering again. Reduce water in winter and protect from frost.

COLD HARDINESS: 25°F (–3.9°C)

PROPAGATION: By offsets, leaves

BLOOM TIME: Fall to winter

As the succulent craze began, 'Black Prince' quickly jumped to the forefront of one of the most popular. The dark-hued rosettes of this relatively frost-hardy succulent contrast beautifully with the gray and silvery tones of other Echeverias. The nearly black color of this favorite comes from *Echeveria affinis*, known as the "black echeveria." The crossing of *E. affinis* with *E. shaviana* created 'Black Prince', thanks to hybridizer Frank Reinelt in California. It offsets easily and has a remarkable scarlet-red flower when most echeverias have yellow, orange, or pink.

Echeveria Hybrid

'GORGON'S GROTTO'

FAMILY: Crassulaceae

ORIGIN: Nursery hybrid

CULTURE: Needs porous, well-draining soil with full sun to light shade in the hottest inland locations. Water thoroughly and allow the soil to dry out some before thoroughly watering again. Reduce water in winter and protect from frost.

COLD HARDINESS: 28°F (–2.2°C)

PROPAGATION: By cuttings, leaves

BLOOM TIME: Unknown, likely summer

Renee O'Connell is world famous as a succulent breeder and is especially valued for her amazing echeveria hybrids. 'Gorgon's Gotto' is certainly one of the more outrageous varieties she has created. *Echeveria* 'Enhanced Mauna Loa' was crossed with an unpatented proprietary. The resulting offspring is a large rosette to nearly 1' (0.3 m) across with very satisfactory gray-purple leaves. Caruncles, those unusual patches of warty lumps and bumps seen on the leaves of many echeveria hybrids, are large and pink on 'Gorgon's Grotto', and are an outstanding color contrast to the gray-purple foundation.

Echeveria Hybrid

'NEON BREAKERS'

FAMILY: Crassulaceae

ORIGIN: Nursery hybrid

CULTURE: Needs porous, well-draining soil with full sun to light shade in the hottest inland locations. Water thoroughly and allow the soil to dry out some before thoroughly watering again. Reduce water in winter and protect from frost.

COLD HARDINESS: 28°F (–2.2°C)

PROPAGATION: By cuttings, leaves

BLOOM TIME: Unknown, likely summer

Yet another one of Renee O'Connell's phenomenal hybrids, 'Neon Breakers' is a cross of *E. shaviana* 'Pink Frills' and another proprietary hybrid. It forms rosettes to 8" (20.3 cm) in diameter, eventually producing offsets that form clusters. The rosettes are comprised of many leaves that are a red-violet-mauve color, with neon-pink, extremely crinkly margins. These neon-pink margins seemingly radiate neon light. An outstanding feature of this hybrid is an increased disease and pest resistance, resulting in greater vigor and faster growth. Because of this, it also doesn't go through the typical winter dormancy that echeverias have a tendency to do.

Echeveria Hybrid

'PERLE VON NURNBERG'

FAMILY: Crassulaceae

ORIGIN: Nursery hybrid

CULTURE: Needs porous, well-draining soil with full sun to light shade in the hottest inland locations. Water thoroughly and allow the soil to dry out some before thoroughly watering again. Reduce water in winter and protect from frost.

COLD HARDINESS: 28°F (−2.2°C)

PROPAGATION: By cuttings, leaves

BLOOM TIME: Summer

This hybrid is a favorite among echeveria fans and succulent neophytes as well. It is an old hybrid between *E. gibbiflora* 'Metallica' and *E. elegans*, created by Richard Graessner of Perleberg, Germany, in the 1930s. Its soft, lavender-pink color with somewhat cupped, spoon-shaped leaves have made it a timeless favorite. In summer, 12" (30.5 cm)-tall reddish spikes bear cupped flowers that are coral pink on the exterior with a yellow interior. 'Perle' is about 6" (15.2 cm) wide at maturity, and makes a striking, solitary container specimen.

Echeveria × imbricata

HENS AND CHICKS

FAMILY: Crassulaceae

ORIGIN: Nursery hybrid

CULTURE: Needs porous, well-draining soil with full sun to light shade in the hottest inland locations. Water thoroughly and allow the soil to dry out some before thoroughly watering again. Reduce water in winter and protect from long hard frost.

COLD HARDINESS: 20° to 25°F (–6.7 to –3.9°C)

PROPAGATION: By cuttings, offsets, leaves

BLOOM TIME: Spring to summer

Without much doubt, this is the most often seen and grown of echeverias, truly a testament to a very old hybrid (1870s) with great appeal. These flat, 6"- to 8"(15.2 cm to 20.3 cm)-wide rosettes are an attractive blue-gray and very prolific. The proverbial "hens" are quickly popping out "chicks" around them, creating impressive spreading clumps or colonies. Spring and summer bring on branched, arching flower spikes with clusters of red and yellow flowers that are enjoyed by hummingbirds.

Echeveria × imbricata 'Compton Carousel'

VARIEGATED HENS AND CHICKS

FAMILY: Crassulaceae

ORIGIN: Garden hybrid

CULTURE: Needs a porous, well-draining soil with full sun to light shade in the hottest inland locations. Water thoroughly and allow the soil to dry out some before thoroughly watering again. Reduce water in winter and protect from long, hard frost.

COLD HARDINESS: 25°F (–6.7°C)

PROPAGATION: Cuttings, offsets, leaves

BLOOM TIME: Summer

This is an astonishingly beautiful echeveria that forms tight rosettes with exceptional coloration. The short, wide, and slightly cupped blue-gray leaves sport a wide cream-colored margin with a blush of pink on older leaves, particularly during cooler temperatures in winter. Readily producing offsets, it will in time produce a dense, slightly mounding clump. Like many spontaneous garden hybrids, this gem has somewhat murky parentage with various theories that can be further researched if desired.

Echeveria nodulosa

PAINTED ECHEVERIA

FAMILY: Crassulaceae

ORIGIN: Mexico

CULTURE: Needs porous, well-draining soil with cool full sun to light shade in the hottest inland locations. Water thoroughly and allow the soil to dry out some before thoroughly watering again. Reduce water in winter and protect from frost.

COLD HARDINESS: 25°F (–6.7°C)

PROPAGATION: By cuttings, leaves

BLOOM TIME: Summer

This is a gem among *Echeveria* species. Growing more like a small sub-shrub, it has a branching habit 1' to 2' (0.3 to 0.6 m) tall and 3' to 4' (0.9 to 1.2 m) wide. The stems support 5" (38.1 cm) -wide rosettes at their ends, causing the branches to arch and lay over with time and added rosette weight. The leaves are roughly a shade of pistachio green and painted with red margins and red longitudinal patterns on the top surfaces. The cupped leaves also have a distinct keel on the underside and it is likewise painted red along its length. There is also a light speckling of red all over the leaves, top and bottom. A flower spike nearly 2' (0.6 m) tall in summer bears pale yellow flowers that are often marked with red. This species is beginning to make a mark, adding its unique patterns and color to new hybrids.

Echeveria runyonii

'TOPSY TURVY'

FAMILY: Crassulaceae

ORIGIN: Mexico

CULTURE: Needs porous, well-draining soil with full sun to light shade in the hottest inland locations. Water thoroughly and allow the soil to dry out some before thoroughly watering again. Reduce water in winter and protect from frost.

COLD HARDINESS: 30°F (–1.1°C)

PROPAGATION: By offsets, cuttings, leaves

BLOOM TIME: Summer

This fast-growing, rosette-forming succulent has pale blue-gray leaves that curve upward and are strongly inversely keeled on the lower surface, with leaf tips pointing in toward the center of the plant. The normal form of *E. runyonii* is a typical flat-leafed rosette like most other echeverias. 'Topsy Turvy' is beautifully colored a pale blue-gray. It almost gives it a "chrysanthemum" appearance. As an added bonus, the plant produces offsets profusely and easily forms a colony.

Echinocactus grusonii

GOLDEN BARREL, MOTHER-IN-LAW'S CUSHION

FAMILY: Cactaceae

ORIGIN: Mexico

CULTURE: Needs porous, well-draining soil with full sun. Water thoroughly and allow the soil to dry out before thoroughly watering again. Reduce water in winter.

COLD HARDINESS: 15° to 20°F (–9.4 to –6.7°C)

PROPAGATION: By seed, offsets

BLOOM TIME: Spring to summer

Along with the giant saguaro of the Sonoran Desert, the golden barrel is the other quintessential cactus that instantly says "desert" to most people. This amazing ball is armed with thousands of slightly curved, very stiff, and very sharp bright yellow spines. A ring or crown of bright yellow flowers encircles the top of larger mature specimens. The oldest specimens can reach about 35 years old and by that time have grown upright to approximately 3' (0.9 m) tall and taken on a columnar appearance. The plant is cold tolerant if it is not for a very prolonged period. There are various cultivars, and *Echinocactus grusonii* var. *albispina* is particularly attractive with snow-white spines.

Echinopsis chamaecereus

PEANUT CACTUS

FAMILY: Cactaceae

ORIGIN: Argentina

CULTURE: Best in a pot with well-drained soil in a sunny spot. Needs a period of cool rest in winter for best flower production.

COLD HARDINESS: 20°F (–6.7°C)

PROPAGATION: By offsets

BLOOM TIME: Late spring

With the peanut cactus, plant enthusiasts have taken a nearly extinct species and made it one of the most popular and common cactuses in the world. *Echinopsis chamaecereus* was collected and described at the beginning of the twentieth century but has never been found in the wild again. It's a small cactus with finger-like columns and bright scarlet flowers that are often produced in profuse quantities. As the cactus ages, the columns eventually become woody and spineless. This plant looks great in pots and hanging baskets. A pure yellow mutation also exists and is quite popular. Because it has no chlorophyll, the plant can't make its own food and so must be grafted onto another cactus with chlorophyll in order to survive.

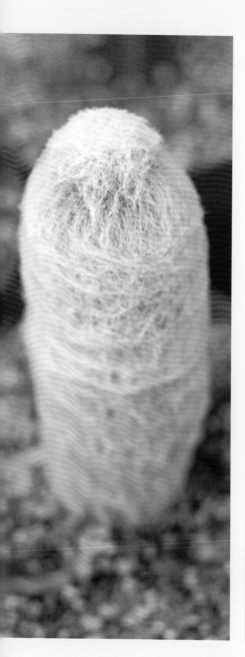

Espostoa lanata

PERUVIAN OLD MAN CACTUS, SNOW POLE CACTUS

FAMILY: Cactaceae

ORIGIN: Southern Ecuador, northern Peru

CULTURE: Water thoroughly when soil is dry to the touch, but water should be infrequent in cold winter months and soil should not remain waterlogged.

COLD HARDINESS: 25°F (–3.9°C) (for brief periods, prefers no frost)

PROPAGATION: By seed

BLOOM TIME: Late spring or early summer

Hairy cactuses are always popular with collectors, and this one is no exception. *Espostoa lanata* is a columnar cactus with dense white hair and golden spines. The woolly hairs from the stem have been used for pillow filling in Peru. It is native to mountainous regions at elevations of 4,000'–7,000' (1219 m to 2134 m). In time, it will form a branched, tree-like columnar to 6' (1.8 m) ded pumice or perlite for extra drainage. Espostoa requires bright light to produce dense hairs, but, as a former mountain dweller, does not care for extremely high temperatures. It is best to refrain from watering on cloudy, overcast, or very humid days as well. As the plant matures, it develops a cephalium (a dense growth of wool-like spines on one side of the column near the growing tip). White to purple flowers are borne from this hairy growth.

Euphorbia anoplia

ZIPPER PLANT

FAMILY: Euphorbiaceae

ORIGIN: South Africa

CULTURE: Light shade and keep dry in winter (November–March).

COLD HARDINESS: 40°F (4.5°C)

PROPAGATION: By stem cuttings, seed

BLOOM TIME: Spring to summer

Euphorbia anoplia, native to South Africa, is a short, chunky green plant forming dense clusters. The common name, zipper plant, comes from the patterns along margins of angled stems that resemble a zipper. Like many euphorbias, it responds well to warmth and its active growth period is late spring and the summer months. Plants develop into a colony of leafless ribbed columns. The columns are usually somewhat variegated to green with small dark burgundy flowers at the column tips during the growing season. Zipper plants do well in fast-draining rock gardens and containers. For best appearance, protect from frost that can scar or discolor the stems. Be cautious with irritating sap if handling.

Euphorbia flanaganii

MEDUSA'S HEAD

FAMILY: Euphorbiaceae

ORIGIN: Eastern Cape of South Africa

CULTURE: Can tolerate light shade. Water sparingly during the summer and keep mostly dry in winter. Good drainage is essential.

COLD HARDINESS: 32°F (0°C)

PROPAGATION: By seed, cuttings

BLOOM TIME: Sporadically everblooming

Euphorbia flanaganii is one member of an intriguing group of succulents known as the "medusoid euphorbias" because of their form, which consists of a central head sprouting numerous snakelike arms resembling locks of hairs. The central stem merges into roots and forms a tuberous body with branches radiating from it. Gazing down upon a large specimen presents the viewer with a sunflower-like display. This is another instance of nature's living patterns as a Fibonacci spiral. A specimen plant is a delight to see. When in full bloom, each snaky finger is covered with fragrant yellow flowers and the cluster is ethereal. It adapts well to being planted in containers, window boxes, and hanging baskets.

Euphorbia flanaganii cristata

GREEN CORAL

FAMILY: Euphorbiaceae

ORIGIN: Nursery-produced cultivar

CULTURE: Needs good drainage. Water sparingly during the summer months and keep on the dry side in winter.

COLD HARDINESS: 35°F (1.7°C)

PROPAGATION: By cuttings

BLOOM TIME: Does not bloom

Here is a phenomenal, nursery-found cristation. Unlike monstrose varieties of plants, where the differentiation from normal growth is due to a genetic mutation, crested growth can occur on normal plants. Causes for the aberrant growth are not specifically known, but may result from variances in light intensity or mechanical damage. Crested plants may have some areas that exhibit normal growth, and a cresting plant that looks like a brain may revert back for no apparent reason. Normal growth should be pruned out and only the crested part of the plant should remain or the normal growth may overcome the crest. Green coral is a fantastic crested form of euphorbia that forms a tight mound 4" to 5" (10.2 cm to 12.7 cm) high by up to 12" (30.5 cm) wide. The stems fold back and forth in a ribbon pattern to give the plant a bizarre coral or brain-like form. As the plant ages, it will also form a very nice caudiciform base. The tight, compact form of this euphorbia provides a conversation piece for the mixed potted succulent garden or as a beautiful solitary specimen. It also works well in the ground in mild areas, assuming the soil is fast draining. If grown in high light, the plant will develop a handsome maroon ribbon along the top of the crest.

Euphorbia mammillaris variegata
CORN COB EUPHORBIA

FAMILY: Euphorbiaceae
ORIGIN: Tropical and southern Africa
CULTURE: Easy to grow in well-drained soil in half or full sun.
COLD HARDINESS: 45°F (7.2°C)
PROPAGATION: By seed, cuttings
BLOOM TIME: Late winter to early summer

Euphorbia mammillaris is a plant species endemic to the Cape Province of South Africa. The common name reflects the growth habit of forming stems in rows that look like corn cobs. They are a light green with dark green hints and tips that turn pink in the sun. Active growth occurs in the late spring and summer months. Water thoroughly when the soil is dry to the touch during this period. Bright light is mandatory to keep this succulent looking its best. It needs to rest in winter and should be given less water during this period. As with all euphorbias, handle with care.

Euphorbia milii

CROWN OF THORNS

FAMILY: Euphorbiaceae

ORIGIN: Madagascar

CULTURE: Grow in full sun to light shade. Needs porous, well-draining soil, and water occasionally, allowing the soil to dry slightly before watering again. One of the easiest euphorbias to grow.

COLD HARDINESS: 25°F (–3.9°C) for brief periods

PROPAGATION: By seed, cuttings

BLOOM TIME: Year-round

The common name refers to the belief by some that the crown of thorns worn by Jesus Christ at the crucifixion may have been made from the stems of this plant. Indeed, historical evidence suggests that the plant may have been introduced to the Middle East prior to the birth of Christ. *Euphorbia milii* is a woody, succulent shrub that has bright green leaves and thick, sharp, black thorns that cover its water-storing branches and stems. In Madagascar, this shrub typically grows in a sprawling form to 5' to 6' (1.5 m to 1.8 m). While these features alone still make for an interesting succulent, the flowers raise the interest to fascination. Similar to poinsettias, the colorful part of the crown of thorns "flower" is not petals in the usual sense, but leaf-like bracts of poinsettia-red color. The plant has been beloved by gardeners for ages, but the new hybrids from Thailand have made the plant trendy. The Thai hybrids include plants with larger flower clusters approaching hydrangeas in showiness and come in a wide range of color combinations. They have more of an upright form that does not become a twisted mass like the species. The leaves tend to be larger and brighter. These hybrids tend to be a little more frost tender than the species.

Euphorbia obesa Hybrid

BASEBALL PLANT, SEA URCHIN

FAMILY: Euphorbiaceae

ORIGIN: Northern Cape region of South Africa

CULTURE: Prefers sun, but can tolerate moderate shade. Good drainage is essential. Water sparingly during the summer and keep dry in winter.

COLD HARDINESS: 25°F (–3.9°C) if roots are kept dry

PROPAGATION: By seed, cuttings if available

BLOOM TIME: Summer

Plants that mimic objects or other creatures are often decimated in the wild as collectors remove them from their habitat. Fortunately, wild harvesting of this plant was stopped early in the twentieth century and it survives quite nicely. *Euphorbia obesa* is a captivating plant with a spherical grayish green body with transverse bands of different shades of green. Often, especially in bright light, these bands can be an attractive contrasting purplish bronze. The peculiar, almost ball-shaped dwarf succulent makes a great conversation piece. It can grow to 8" (20.3 cm) in height with a diameter of 3.5" (9 cm). It is a single-stemmed, unbranched, firm-bodied plant. In younger plants, the stem is usually eight-angled, grooved, and a rounded sea urchin–like shape. As the plant ages, it elongates and becomes more cylindrical. The baseball plant also has a tapering taproot, so grow in deeper rather than more shallow containers. This hybrid variety grows slightly more pointed with deeper rib sections and is prolific at creating offsets. The current thought is that *Euphorbia heptagona* is involved in this cross.

Euphorbia polygona 'Snowflake'

AFRICAN MILK BARREL, SNOWFLAKE EUPHORBIA

FAMILY: Euphorbiaceae

ORIGIN: South Africa

CULTURE: Porous soil with adequate drainage.

COLD HARDINESS: 25°F (−3.9°C)

PROPAGATION: By cuttings, offsets

BLOOM TIME: Year-round

'Snowflake' is a selected cultivar of the species *E. polygona*. Rather than the dull-green stems of the species, this cultivar boasts a chalky-white body and has fewer spiny protuberances, if any. Reports are that only a single 'Snowflake' was ever found in the Eastern Cape province of South Africa. All plants now marketed are descendants of that one specimen. Many new hybrids have been created using 'Snowflake', as it tends to pass on excellent genetics for attractive plants. It responds well to warmth, with its active growth period in the late spring and summer months. The plant requires bright light for best appearance, and should be given a winter resting period, during which less water should be given. Protect from frost.

Euphorbia tirucalli 'Firesticks'

FIRE STICKS, STICKS OF FIRE, RED PENCIL TREE

FAMILY: Euphorbiaceae

ORIGIN: South Africa

CULTURE: Full sun to partial shade; well-draining, porous soil; and thorough watering, allowing the soil to dry before repeating. Reduce water in winter.

COLD HARDINESS: 30°F (−1.1°C)

PROPAGATION: By cuttings

BLOOM TIME: Insignificant spring flowers

A native of arid South Africa, this striking succulent is an ideal specimen plant for containers or for use as a landscape feature in frost-free climates. Multiple fire-red stems, resembling small pencils or sticks, grow from the base of the plant. The red stems often show shades of pink, orange, or yellow, and the color is more vivid during the cooler months of late fall though winter. The colors revert with the coming of summer heat and it becomes an attractive green succulent. 'Firesticks' is extremely heat tolerant, drought tolerant, and virtually pest free. The plant is a form of *Euphorbia tirucalli*, which can grow to 25' tall by 8' to 10' wide (7.6 m tall by 2.4 to 3 m wide), but 'Firesticks' lacks the chlorophyll of the species and will probably stay under 8' (2.4 m) in height. Remember that the milky sap is toxic. Be careful not to touch your eyes when handling this plant, as intense burning can occur.

Euphorbia trigona 'Royal Red'

ROYAL RED MILK TREE

FAMILY: Euphorbiaceae

ORIGIN: Western Africa

CULTURE: Porous soil with adequate drainage. Water thoroughly when soil is dry to the touch during the active growing season.

COLD HARDINESS: 40°F (4.4°C)

PROPAGATION: By cuttings

BLOOM TIME: Never been known to flower

Euphorbia trigona is a frost-tender, evergreen succulent. The stems have three winglike angles and carry short, sharp spines as well as leaves. Eventually, the plant grows into a dense, compact branched shrub 4' to 6' (1.2 m to 1.8 m) in height. 'Royal Red' is a cultivar of the species with stems and leaves that are flushed purplish red. The leaves are usually darker red and the stems can be flecked with red shading to magenta. Excellent in bright areas of the home or office, or as a patio plant in more temperate regions. Responds well to warmth, with its active growth period in the late spring and summer months. Plants may survive brief freezing, but often permanent scarring will occur.

Faucaria tigrina

TIGER JAWS, SHARK JAWS

FAMILY: Aizoaceae

ORIGIN: Eastern Cape Province, South Africa

CULTURE: Water moderately from the middle of summer to the end of winter. Keep partially shaded from hot summer sun and provide maximum light the rest of the year.

COLD HARDINESS: 30°F (–1.1°C)

PROPAGATION: Seeds or rhizome division

BLOOM TIME: Autumn to early winter

The tiger jaws plant is undoubtedly one of the world's most popular succulents. It is an intriguing succulent with soft white teeth along the edges of its fat leaves, and it is a plant that attracts most children. With a little imagination, the leaves are reminiscent of miniature alligator jaws, but it reminds some of an obese Venus flytrap. The long, white, threadlike teeth structures are actually special adaptations that help collect water vapor from the surrounding air and direct it down toward the roots of the plant. Fog blowing in from the coast provides moisture to help plants survive the hot, arid climate of the Eastern Cape. In the garden, tiger jaws slowly sucker and spread in a circular pattern, forming rosettes of thick, fleshy, three-angled grayish green leaves. Large, silky, yellow, daisy-like flowers that open in the afternoon are a surprising bonus in the fall. The genus *Faucaria* is part of the family Aizoaceae, which includes the various forms of plants known as "mimicry plants." *Faucaria tigrina* prefers a soil with less organic material; extra pumice or perlite provides excellent drainage essential for growing these types of plants.

Fenestraria aurantiaca

BABY TOES, WINDOW PLANT

FAMILY: Aizoaceae

ORIGIN: South Africa

CULTURE: Full to part sun. Prefers sandy soil; water sparingly at all times to avoid root rot and split leaves. Keep on the dry side in the summer.

COLD HARDINESS: 25°F (–3.9°C)

PROPAGATION: Division or seed

BLOOM TIME: Midwinter to early spring

Fenestraria or Baby Toes are very unusual plants from the deserts of South Africa. These plants belong to a large family of Aizoaceae, which includes plants known for their ability to camouflage with their environment. Baby Toes have fingerlike leaves in upright clusters. Each "finger" has a translucent "window" at the tip. It is through this window that the harsh African sunlight is filtered to enable photosynthesis without burning the plant. Often, in habitat, only these windows are visible above the quartz sand. Prefers a soil with less organic material; extra pumice or perlite provides the excellent drainage that is essential to these types of plants. Baby Toes requires bright light to prevent the leaves from "stretching." Water thoroughly when soil is dry to the touch, because it will not tolerate waterlogged soils. These plants are somewhat frost tolerant, but protection is advisable to prevent scarring.

Ferocactus latispinus

DEVIL'S TONGUE BARREL CACTUS, CANDY CACTUS

FAMILY: Cactaceae

ORIGIN: Central and Southern Mexico

CULTURE: Needs full sun and well-draining, porous soil. Provide thorough watering, allowing the soil to dry during the summer growing period.

COLD HARDINESS: 30°F (–1.1°C)

PROPAGATION: Seeds

BLOOM TIME: Late summer to early autumn

The common name of Candy Cactus comes from the fact that the plant is used to make sweets. The middle is cored out and soaked in sugar, then chopped up and eaten. This beautiful cactus is put to much better use in the garden. The bold spines create a striking appearance contrasted to the brilliant green of the plant's main body. While it is slow with growing to start, *Ferocactus latispinus* does well under cultivation, eventually forming a globular shape that is about 10" to 16" (25.4 to 40.6 cm) in diameter. Well-maintained plants can flower as small as 4" (10.2 cm) in diameter with pinkish purple or yellow flowers.

Furcraea macdougallii
MACDOUGALL'S HEMP

FAMILY: Asparagaceae
ORIGIN: Oaxaca, Mexico
CULTURE: Prefers full sun and is extremely drought tolerant.
COLD HARDINESS: 25°F (–3.9°C)
PROPAGATION: From bulbils and seeds
BLOOM TIME: Late spring to early summer

Here is definitely one of the most spectacular and dramatic plants in the Agave family. This tree, furcraea, becomes an impressive landscape plant that is prized by both designers and collectors. At about 15' (4.6 m) in height, it is certainly the tallest member of the family. The trunk is upright with blue-green leaves that are toothed, long, thin, and tapering to a soft point. The backs of the leaves have a soft, sandpapery feel. Unlike most plants in the Agave family, this plant does not sucker, but grows in a solitary, upright fashion to eventually develop a woody trunk up to 15' (4.6 m) in height. From afar, it resembles a small palm tree. Like most Agaves, it is monocarpic (dies after flowering). The flower spike is one of the wonders of the plant kingdom. Hundreds of greenish, white-edged blossoms are borne on a spike that can reach to 20' (6.1 m) above the plant! Small bulbils are produced all along the flowering stalk and fall to the ground, where they can easily be rooted.

Gasteraloe 'Green Ice'
GREEN ICE GASTERALOE, PEARL ALOE, LIZARD TAIL

FAMILY: Asphodelaceae
ORIGIN: Nursery hybrid between *Aloe variegata* and *Gasteria* 'Little Warty'
CULTURE: Requires light shade to shade. They prefer a very porous potting mix to increase drainage. During the hot summer months, the soil should be kept moist but not overly wet.
COLD HARDINESS: 32°F (0°C)
PROPAGATION: Offshoots or leaf cuttings
BLOOM TIME: Continually, but heaviest in midwinter

Gasteraloe 'Green Ice' is a fat-leafed hybrid succulent raised from the cross noted above, so it has a plant body intermediate in form between an Aloe and a Gasteria. With gray-green leaves striped with deeper green and spotted with white, it becomes an instant attraction. The leaf margins are wide and unmarked. The first offsets from the center of the plant arise with a leaf arrangement in a flat plane, but as the offset grows, it begins to produce leaves that approach a whorl. Its almost everblooming greenish pink flower spikes and its ease of care are reasons for the popularity of the plant. Because it is a bigeneric cross, it is a "mule" that doesn't produce viable seed, but is easily multiplied by separating the offshoots.

Gymnocalycium mihanovichii 'Hibotan'

MOON CACTUS, RUBY BALL

FAMILY: Cactaceae

ORIGIN: Paraguay

CULTURE: Needs a porous, well-draining soil. Water occasionally, allowing the soil to dry slightly before watering again. Keep mostly dry in winter.

COLD HARDINESS: 40°F (4.4°C)

PROPAGATION: By grafting

BLOOM TIME: Mid-spring to midsummer

Moon cactuses undeniably have an out-of-this-world appearance. They don't look natural because they are not. These neon-colored cactuses first made their way into Western markets in the 1960s and began to appear in mass-market outlets in the 1980s as thousands of plants were produced in Asia for export. The brightly colored cactuses are the outcome of genetic mutations. The resulting variations lack chlorophyll and the body color manifests as dazzling pink, orange, yellow, or red rather than the typical green. No chlorophyll means that the plants are incapable of producing the necessary chemical changes that are involved in photosynthesis and therefore cannot continue to grow and thrive in nature. However, if the plants are grafted onto fast-growing plants such as hylocereus, the "base" plant can provide the necessary chlorophyll for the "upper" plant to thrive. Moon cactus is an excellent subject for windowsill culture. It requires porous cactus soil with adequate drainage and prefers filtered light or shade with ample airflow. Water thoroughly when the soil is dry to the touch. Protect from frost, because the base of the plant is a tropical species of cactus.

Hatiora salicornioides
DRUNKARD'S DREAM, BOTTLE CACTUS, MISTLETOE CACTUS

FAMILY: Cactaceae

ORIGIN: Brazil

CULTURE: Partial shade; appreciates more organic matter in soil medium than most terrestrial cactuses.

COLD HARDINESS: 40°F (4.4°C)

PROPAGATION: By stem cuttings

BLOOM TIME: Late winter to early spring

Hatiora salicornioides is most often called drunkard's dream, but is sometimes called mistletoe cactus because of the white berries that follow the golden-yellow flowers. After flowering, the plant goes through a period of rest until the end of spring. The bottle-shaped leaf segments are produced on stems that are compact enough to create a full and appealing specimen. It doesn't take long to make an excellent windowsill pot plant or an impressive hanging basket. The plant is epiphytic and grows in the crotches of trees in the rainforest or occasionally on rocks, so it thrives best in fast-draining soils. While it naturally grows in the cooler shade of trees, bottle cactus also tolerates the extreme heat of the desert, provided that it is not exposed to direct sun.

Haworthia fasciata
ZEBRA CACTUS

FAMILY: Aloaceae

ORIGIN: South Africa

CULTURE: Prefers filtered, bright light. Needs very porous soil with excellent drainage.

COLD HARDINESS: 30°F (–1.1°C)

PROPAGATION: By offsets, seed

BLOOM TIME: Mid-spring

Haworthias are easy to grow and are little jewels of various shapes and colors. *Haworthia fasciata*, native to South Africa, is an upright, slender rosette with tapering incurved dark green leaves covered with silvery white raised "pearls" that connect to form bands that give the impression of zebra stripes. Because of their relatively small size, they make great plants for indoor gardens. The flowers occur on a spike of 10" to 15" (25.4 to 38.1 cm) in length. Blooms are a whitish color with light reddish brown bands, and are open on two lips. Haworthias do have rather high nutrient requirements compared to other succulents. Add a water-soluble fertilizer at half strength once a month in spring and summer months to keep the plants looking their best.

Haworthia retusa

STAR CACTUS

FAMILY: Asphodelaceae

ORIGIN: Cape Province, South Africa

CULTURE: Adapts to moderate sun or shade; needs well-draining porous soil and thorough watering, allowing the soil to dry before repeating. Reduce water in winter.

COLD HARDINESS: 25°F (−3.9°C)

PROPAGATION: By division, offsets, seed, or leaf cuttings

BLOOM TIME: Late spring to summer

Haworthia retusa is a popular succulent that forms shiny, green, star-shaped rosettes, and was introduced into cultivation at the beginning of the eighteenth century. The top surface of its smooth leaves house nearly translucent windows that illuminate the interior photosynthetic areas of the leaves—a particular curiosity for botanists. These are called "window leaves" and represent an acclimation to desert conditions. In its native habitat, the star cactus is often buried deep in the ground with only the window leaves visible. Haworthias make easy-care house plants and they can be interesting contributions to dry rock gardens as well.

Haworthia truncata

HORSE'S TEETH

FAMILY: Asphodelaceae

ORIGIN: South Africa

CULTURE: Grows best in sandy/gritty soil and requires good drainage, as it is prone to root rot. Partial sun to shady conditions.

COLD HARDINESS: 32°F (0°C)

PROPAGATION: By division, offsets, seed, or leaf cuttings

BLOOM TIME: Fall to winter

As with many haworthias, horse's teeth is one of the strange and wonderful oddities of the botanical world. It, too, has the phenomenon of "window leaves," which allow a leaf buried in the soil to still receive the sunlight necessary for photosynthesis, transmitting it from the window through the clear, juicy inner tissue of the leaf to the green outer layer. Being hunkered down in the soil also offers the plant protection from desiccation and from browsing by animals. Under cultivation, this succulent tends to grow above soil, albeit quite slowly. This better displays the unusual leaf form that earns the plant the Afrikaans name of *perderande,* or horse's teeth. Japanese breeders who often become obsessed with certain groups of plants have focused on developing a number of fascinating cultivars of *H. truncate.* This succulent is certainly one of the best for indoor culture.

Hylocereus undatus

PITAYA, DRAGON FRUIT, NIGHT-BLOOMING CEREUS

FAMILY: Cactaceae

ORIGIN: Central America

CULTURE: Well-drained soil in full coastal sun, but protect in hot inland areas.

COLD HARDINESS: 32°F (0°C)

PROPAGATION: By seed or stem cuttings

BLOOM TIME: Late summer–early fall

Hylocereus undatus is one of the most rampant species in the cactus family. Its fleshy, three-angled, jointed stems sprawl up to 30' (9.1 m) over other plants and produce fibrous, aerial roots that cling to any available surface. In their natural habitat, support is provided by trees, shrubs, and rocks. The plant actually grows more like a tropical vine. From late spring into fall, the fragrant, large, white, bell-shaped flowers appear at dusk and last only for one night. In cold climates, all-night parties (for plant nerds, of course) are often held to behold the unfurling of the fragrantly exotic flowers. After the flowers are pollinated, they are followed with the large oval-shaped fruit that can weigh as much as 2 pounds (0.9 kg). Dragon fruit production is becoming popular worldwide in accommodating climates. Plant in a well-draining soil. Irrigate only a small amount (shallowly) but regularly in summer, including areas where aerial roots may be attached. This plant requires a near frost-free climate to produce fruits.

Kalanchoe 'Houghton's Hybrid', 'Pink Butterflies'

PINK BUTTERFLIES, PINK SPARKLER

FAMILY: Crassulaceae

ORIGIN: Madagascar

CULTURE: Bright, sunny locations, especially in the summer growing season. Indoors, during the winter, consider a south-facing window.

COLD HARDINESS: 35°F (1.7°C)

PROPAGATION: By leaf or stem cuttings

BLOOM TIME: Fall

"Incredibly beautiful" is not an exaggeration when describing this plant. Both parents of the original hybrid are viviparous, meaning they produce hundreds (seems like millions) of tiny plantlets on their leaves that readily fall and root with little to no effort. While this is an easy way to propagate, these plants can quickly become invasive and take over the garden. *Kalanchoe* 'Pink Butterflies' is an astonishingly colorful variegated sport of a cross known as 'Houghton's Hybrid', a combination of *K. daigremontiana* × *K. delagoensis*. This was a fortuitous mutation for succulent lovers. Not only is 'Pink Butterflies' incredibly beautiful, but it is also not one bit invasive. It still produces abundant quantities of tiny pink butterfly-like plantlets on its leaves, but because they lack chlorophyll, they have lost their ability to grow from plantlets. The colors of the plantlets become more intense as the amount of sun they receive increases. Provide a porous soil with adequate drainage, water thoroughly when the soil is dry to the touch, and protect from frost.

Kalanchoe Hybrid
'BORDEAUX'

FAMILY: Crassulaceae   **ORIGIN:** Nursery-grown hybrid
CULTURE: Needs a porous, well-draining soil with full sun to light shade in the hottest inland locations. Water thoroughly and allow the soil to dry out somewhat before thoroughly watering again. Protect from frost.
COLD HARDINESS: 30° to 35°F (−1.1° to −1.7°C)
PROPAGATION: Cuttings   **BLOOM TIME:** Spring

'Bordeaux' has an easily branching, upright, compact habit that grows to about 1' (0.3 m) tall and wide. Relatively fast growing, it sports leaves with a distinctive toothed margin toward the leaf tip. These leaves are a rich green that is drenched in a deep burgundy-violet. In cooler temperatures, this coloring is noticeably intensified, creating an even more eye-catching display. Clusters of small bell-shaped flowers appear in spring. Unusually, the outer surface of the petals is often divided longitudinally into lobes of two colors, a shade of pink and a shade of apricot. This hybrid cultivar is another creation from Renee O'Connell of San Diego, California.

Kalanchoe luciae
FLAPJACKS, PADDLE PLANT

FAMILY: Crassulaceae   **ORIGIN:** South Africa
CULTURE: Plant in full sun to light shade.
COLD HARDINESS: 29°F (−1.7°C)
PROPAGATION: From leaf cuttings or cuttings of plantlets that form on the flowering stem
BLOOM TIME: Late winter to early spring

Whether or not this succulent evokes flapjacks or paddles, it is a desirable addition to any collection. The leaves are covered in a dusky gray, and the leaf margin takes on a reddish hue during cooler winter months. The red tones only appear if the plant is grown in bright light; otherwise, the leaves remain uniformly green. At blossom time (which occurs after three or four seasons), a single long stem, from 2' to 3' (0.6 m to 0.9 m), bearing clusters of pale yellow tubular flowers appears, after which the plant dies. The plant produces numerous offsets throughout its life, however, ensuring that there are always replacements. Be sure to protect them from snail and slug damage, which will cause permanent disfigurement.

Kalanchoe tomentosa

PANDA PLANT, TEDDY BEAR PLANT

FAMILY: Crassulaceae

ORIGIN: Madagascar

CULTURE: Prefers a porous soil with adequate drainage. Water thoroughly when soil is dry to the touch. Protect from frost.

COLD HARDINESS: 29°F (−1.7°C)

PROPAGATION: Stem cuttings, leaf cuttings

BLOOM TIME: Spring

Panda plant is as adorable as its namesake. Its captivating, furry blue-gray leaves are covered in tiny white hairs with brown spots on the leaves' edges. It's a perfect plant to interest children in gardening—touching the leaves can be as irresistible as popping bubble wrap. The fuzziness of the leaves has a practical use in this plant's natural habitat too. Because of its native arid environment, *K. tomentosa* must conserve what little water it can absorb from the soil. The dense mat of hairs growing from the leaves retards the movement of air directly across the leaf surface, which reduces water transpiration. In addition, the light silvery leaves reflect light, reducing the chances of the leaves overheating. 'Chocolate Soldier' is a common cultivar with leaves that are more red-brown around the edges and thinner and longer than the standard species. It also grows somewhat faster and has something of a clumping habit.

Leuchtenbergia principis

PRISM CACTUS, AGAVE CACTUS

FAMILY: Cactaceae   **ORIGIN:** North-Central Mexico

CULTURE: Has a strong taproot; grow in a deep pot. Lack of water will make the tips of the leaves yellow, but too much water will make it rot.

COLD HARDINESS: 30°F (−1.1°C)

PROPAGATION: Seeds   **BLOOM TIME:** Intermittent from spring to fall

A true cactus that bears an uncanny resemblance to an agave or aloe, this strange-looking plant is the only member of its genus. With long and sharply angled tubercles (swellings that look like the leaves) tipped with harmless papery spines, it is amazing that this is actually a cactus. Prism cactus is relatively slow growing, but can eventually grow up to 2' (0.6 m) tall, with a cylindrical stem that becomes bare and corky at the base as the plant ages. While bizarreness is the main attraction, the plant also has significant flowers. Large, funnel-shaped, fragrant yellow blooms are produced from the areole at the tip of the new tubercles on mature plants (at least four to five years old). Overall, the agave cactus is a reasonably easy plant to care for under the general regime for most other succulents. Sunlight, however, is extremely important to this plant's healthy appearance—if it is grown exclusively indoors, it may never thrive. In cold climates, plants will benefit from positioning outside during the warmer months of spring through early fall.

Lithops spp.

LIVING STONES

FAMILY: Aizoaceae   **ORIGIN:** South Africa

CULTURE: Coarse, well-drained substrate is a necessity. Water only in fall; the rest of the year, water only to keep plant from shriveling.

COLD HARDINESS: 40°F (4.4°C)

PROPAGATION: By seed   **BLOOM TIME:** Fall to winter

Widely known as living stones, lithops are some of the world's most remarkable plants. The genus name derives from two Greek words that literally translate as "stone face," and they avoid being eaten by animals with their ability to blend in with surrounding rocks. They even eluded Western discovery until 1811, when naturalist William John Burchell wrote of them, "On picking up from the stony ground what was supposed a curiously shaped pebble, it proved to be a plant." Ever since, lithops have been avidly sought by collectors. With subtle colors of gray, brown, rust, green, and pink, and intricately designed markings, these plants become some of the most seductive members of the succulent family. Because the plants are so small, it's easy to grow a collection on a sunny windowsill, a patio table, or even under grow lights. Flowers that dwarf the plants are produced in the fall; they should be allowed to go drier in winter, as these new growths draw water from the old leaves. Only provide sufficient moisture to keep the root hairs alive, or else they will die and the plant will be unable to absorb any water. When the new plant bodies are forming, the old leaves become soft and flimsy and begin to shrivel. Eventually, the old leaves dry up, leaving the plant with a perfect set of new ones.

Mammillaria bocasana

SNOWBALL CACTUS, POWDERPUFF
PINCUSHION CACTUS

FAMILY: Cactaceae

ORIGIN: North-Central Mexico around San Luis Potosí

CULTURE: Water regularly in summer if soil is fast-draining. In a container, use a pot with good drainage and a very porous potting medium. Keep dry in winter.

COLD HARDINESS: 15°F (–9.4°C)

PROPAGATION: By seed or offsets

BLOOM TIME: Spring to summer

Powderpuff pincushion cactus is a rather fast-growing and clumping plant that will quickly form large mounds. Its cotton ball–like appearance, coated with silky white hairs, inspired its common name. But don't be fooled! The sharp spines are used to make fishhooks in Mexico. It is quite variable, with many different varieties and forms available in cultivation. This is often one of the first plants to enter the collection of a cactus lover because of its easy cultivation and free-flowering habit. It will survive temperatures well below freezing as long as the soil drains well.

Mammillaria hahniana

OLD LADY CACTUS, BIRTHDAY CAKE CACTUS

FAMILY: Cactaceae   **ORIGIN:** Central Mexico

CULTURE: Easy to grow in porous cactus soil with adequate drainage. Bright light with ample airflow. Water thoroughly when the soil is dry to the touch.

COLD HARDINESS: 25°F (–3.9°C)

PROPAGATION: By seed or offsets

BLOOM TIME: Late spring to early summer

Most of the pincushion group of cactuses flower freely, and the birthday cake cactus is no exception. Cerise flowers are followed by upright red seedpods that stand in a ring around the crown of the cactus, producing the birthday experience. *M. hahniana* is native to Mexico and forms globular stems to 6" (15.2 cm) or more in diameter. The stems are densely covered with white hair and short white spines. The concentric rings of dark pink flowers create a dramatic contrast as they appear amid the white hairs. Although easily found in most garden shops, this species is on the IUCN Red List of near-endangered plants because of the deforestation threat to its habitat in Mexico.

Mammillaria matudae cristata

CRESTED THUMB CACTUS

FAMILY: Cactaceae   **ORIGIN:** Mexico

CULTURE: Needs porous, well-drained soil with full to part sun. Water thoroughly, allowing the soil to dry out before watering again. Reduce watering through winter.

COLD HARDINESS: 25°F (–3.9°C)

PROPAGATION: By cuttings   **BLOOM TIME:** Spring

Cresting of a plant happens when the single, central growing point multiplies either through a natural mutation or because of mechanical damage, such as being eaten by an insect. When these points grow and multiply through natural cell division, they push against one another, forcing the plant's tissues to back up and fanfold in an undulating pattern. This often results in the plant mimicking an appearance similar to the folds of a brain. The crested *Mammillaria matudae* forms thick, fanned folds with characteristic recurved spines that make it surprisingly "touchable" without injury. The spine color is quite variable, from near white to cinnamon, depending on the seedling. Crested forms can be reluctant to bloom, but they might have a spring flush of the typical species' small magenta flowers.

Opuntia cylindrica cristata

AUSTROCYLINDROPUNTIA CYLINDRICA CRISTATA, EMERALD IDOL

FAMILY: Cactaceae   **ORIGIN:** Ecuador, Peru

CULTURE: Needs porous, well-drained soil with full sun. Water thoroughly, allowing the soil to dry out before watering again. Reduce watering through winter.

COLD HARDINESS: 28°F (–2.2°C)

PROPAGATION: By cuttings   **BLOOM TIME:** Unlikely

Similar to other cactus oddities, the cresting of a plant happens when the single, central growing point of a plant multiplies either through a natural mutation or because of mechanical damage. When these points grow and multiply through natural cell division, they push against one another, forcing the plant's tissues to back up and fanfold in an undulating habit. While the normal form is arborescent (tree-like) and up to 12' (3.7 m) tall, the crested form makes an interesting small potted specimen with emerald-green, deep folds and fans. It looks very much like a sea coral, is relatively spineless, and may produce small, succulent, vestigial leaves that are short lived.

Opuntia microdasys

BUNNY EAR CACTUS, POLKA DOT CACTUS

FAMILY: Cactaceae **ORIGIN:** Mexico

CULTURE: Needs porous, well-drained soil with full sun to very light shade. Water thoroughly, allowing the soil to dry out before watering again. Reduce watering through winter and protect from frost.

COLD HARDINESS: 30°F (−1.1°C)

PROPAGATION: By cuttings **BLOOM TIME:** Summer

This is a very attractive beavertail or prickly pear–type of cactus that can be up to 2' (0.6 m) tall and spreads outward 3' to 4' (0.9 to 1.2 m) wide. Pale yellow flowers are followed by oval fruits that can be red to purple in color when ripe, but "buyer beware!" This cactus is not as harmless as its common name would suggest. Although it appears to be spineless and soft to the touch like a dotted swiss fabric, the golden dots on the pads are dense collections of glochids (tiny, highly irritating, loose spines) that easily stick into flesh like fiberglass and are also easily dislodged, becoming airborne and getting into eyes, nasal passages, and the mouth. They don't hurt like a big stiff spine, but become a very irritating, lingering, and dangerous weapon. They can take a long time to be rid of if contracted. Sticky tape is often helpful in dislodging the microspines.

Opuntia quitensis

RED BUTTONS OPUNTIA

FAMILY: Cactaceae **ORIGIN:** Ecuador, Peru

CULTURE: Needs porous, well-drained soil with full sun to very light shade. Water thoroughly, allowing the soil to dry out before watering again. Reduce watering through winter and protect from frost.

COLD HARDINESS: 30°F (−1.1°C)

PROPAGATION: By cuttings **BLOOM TIME:** Summer

This is a charming, different kind of opuntia. Although it has the ability to grow tall, it is usually found as a squat, 12 to 18"(0.3 to 45.7 cm) sprawling plant growing several feet wide. The small pads, rather than being flat, are quite fat, almost inflated in appearance. Small red to orange-red flowers are produced singly at the tip of the uppermost pads. The spines are long but relatively sparse and scattered with no particular pattern.

Opuntia subulata

AUSTROCYLINDROPUNTIA SUBULATA, EVE'S NEEDLE

FAMILY: Cactaceae   **ORIGIN:** Peru

CULTURE: Needs porous, well-drained soil with full sun. Water thoroughly, allowing the soil to dry out before watering again. Reduce watering through winter.

COLD HARDINESS: 20° to 25°F (–6.7 to –3.9°C)

PROPAGATION: By cuttings   **BLOOM TIME:** Summer

Not for the faint of heart! Here is a large, frequently branching, cylindrically stemmed cactus that can reach more than 10' (3.0 m) tall with a spread of more than 12' (3.7 m). It will form a large, dense thicket and is armed with extremely fierce, 2"- to 3"- (5.1 to 7.6 cm) long stiff yellow spines. In times of abundant water and especially on new growth, fleshy 1" to 2" (2.5 cm to 5.1 cm) cylindrical leaves form along the stems and copiously at the stem tips. These dry up and fall off as water becomes scarce. The flowers are an attractive red and a favorite of bees and hummingbirds. Because of its fast growth and heavily armed spines, this opuntia makes an excellent "security plant," often used as a border fence or even planted under windows. It's easily kept in control, as it takes well to pruning to shape.

Opuntia chlorotica var. santa-rita

SANTA RITA PRICKLY PEAR, VIOLET PRICKLY PEAR

FAMILY: Cactaceae

ORIGIN: Arizona, northern Mexico

CULTURE: Needs porous, well-drained soil with full sun. Water thoroughly, allowing the soil to dry out before watering again. Looks best with supplemental water in the hottest months. Reduce watering through winter.

COLD HARDINESS: 25°F (−3.9°C)

PROPAGATION: By cuttings

BLOOM TIME: Late spring

Known for its rich purple color, the pads of this plant are at their best color when stressed due to extremes of heat, cold, or drought. The plant is very frost hardy, often surviving as far north as southern Virginia, where it is deer resistant. The pads lack long spines but are dotted with dense tufts of glochids (tiny, highly irritating spines) that easily stick into flesh like fiberglass. They don't hurt like a big stiff spine, but become a very irritating, lingering problem and can take a long time to be rid of if contracted. Somewhat slow growing, the plant can reach 5' (1.5 m) tall and wide over time. Bright yellow flowers make a remarkable contrast to the violet-purple pads and are followed by edible purple fruits attractive to birds.

Oreocereus celsianus

OLD MAN OF THE ANDES

FAMILY: Cactaceae

ORIGIN: Andes of Argentina, Bolivia, Peru

CULTURE: Needs porous, well-drained soil with full sun. Water thoroughly, allowing the soil to dry out before watering again. Reduce watering through winter.

COLD HARDINESS: 10°F (−12.2°C)

PROPAGATION: By seed

BLOOM TIME: Spring

Popularly known as old man of the Andes, this "Cousin Itt"–type cactus is from the higher altitudes of the Andes of South America. Known for the coat of fluffy white, coarse hairs that cover its entire length, this Oreocereus intrigues both children and adults. In its native habitat, the hairs help protect and shade the plant's green skin from both intense high-altitude sunlight and the occasional cold snap. The main body of the cactus is well armed. The spines are stout, thick, and dirty yellow to reddish brown in color and occur in groups of one to four heavier spines surrounded by seven to nine very sharp radial spines. The spines are nestled deeply into the hairy cloak. At a mature age, this cactus produces flowers, but only at the top of the plant. Each rosy bud sits atop a thick, hairy stem about the size of a man's little finger. Flowers face upward to receive hummingbirds and other insect pollinators.

Pachycereus pringlei

CARDÓN, FALSE SAGUARO, ELEPHANT CACTUS

FAMILY: Cactaceae

ORIGIN: Baja California, and Baja California Sur, Mexico

CULTURE: Needs porous, well-drained soil with full sun. Water thoroughly, allowing the soil to dry out before watering again. Reduce watering through winter and protect from frost.

COLD HARDINESS: 28°F (–2.2°C)

PROPAGATION: By seed

BLOOM TIME: Spring to summer

Pachycereus is the colossus of the cactus family and is able to reach over 60' (18.3 m) tall! It is the Baja California equivalent of the giant saguaro, *Carnegiea gigantea,* of the Sonoran Desert region. Much faster growing than the saguaro, it will branch and put out "arms" at an earlier age than the saguaro, which can take up to 60 years to "branch out." White, funnel-shaped flowers open midday and remain open during the night, when they are fertilized by bats, birds, and insects. The following fruits were eaten by indigenous cultures, but the flesh of this cactus contains alkaloids and may have been used as a psychoactive plant in Mexico, similar to other species in the genus. The fruit pulp and seeds are enjoyed by the local avian population.

Pachycereus schottii

SENITA

FAMILY: Cactaceae

ORIGIN: Southern Arizona and Sonora, Baja California, Mexico

CULTURE: Needs porous, well-drained soil with full sun. Water thoroughly, allowing the soil to dry out before watering again. Reduce watering through winter and protect from frost.

COLD HARDINESS: 35°F (1.7°C)

PROPAGATION: By seed, cuttings

BLOOM TIME: Summer

Senita is the rarest of Arizona's three largest cactuses, after the giant saguaro (*Carnegiea gigantea*) and the organ pipe cactus (*Stenocereus thurberi*). Its scarceness is primarily due to its extreme sensitivity to frost—it will not tolerate it, thus restricting it to very specific locations. Branching from the base and growing to around 20' (6.1 m) tall, it can make hundreds of columns, creating large clumps. Dark, hairy tufts appear near the stem tops. Pink, nocturnal flowers with an unpleasant fragrance appear along the sides of the stems and are pollinated by a specific moth during the night. The variety 'Monstrose', known as the totem pole cactus, is a favorite of collectors and for use in frost-free landscapes. It is spineless, has lost its ribs, and develops random, smooth lumps and bumps.

Pachypodium lamerei

MADAGASCAR PALM

FAMILY: Apocynaceae

ORIGIN: Madagascar

CULTURE: Needs porous, well-drained soil with full sun. Water thoroughly, allowing the soil to dry out before watering again. Reduce watering through winter and protect from frost.

COLD HARDINESS: 35°F (1.7°C)

PROPAGATION: By seed, division

BLOOM TIME: Spring to summer at maturity

As often occurs with common names, this not a palm at all. The Madagascar palm is easy to grow indoors as well as outdoors in frost-free climates. In their natural environment, pachypodiums grow under very hostile conditions. Most thrive in desert conditions and among rocks and gravel, which increase the heat they are exposed to via reflection. This is a popular caudiciform-type plant, meaning it has a swollen trunk that serves as a water reserve in times of drought. The entire trunk is heavily armed with spines in groups of three, and is topped with a crown of lance-shaped, dark green leaves. Only mature plants of some age will bloom, and being related to *Plumeria*, the blossoms are nearly identical in appearance—five petals, white with a yellow center, and pleasantly fragrant. Plants outdoors become deciduous, losing all their leaves when temperatures begin falling below 50°F (10°C). Keep winter watering to an absolute minimum, only maintaining the soil from drying out completely. Indoors, they make an excellent houseplant but need a full south- or west-facing window. Indoor plants are not likely to ever bloom.

Parodia magnifica

BALLOON CACTUS

FAMILY: Cactaceae   **ORIGIN:** Southern Brazil

CULTURE: Needs porous, well-drained soil with full sun. Water thoroughly, allowing the soil to dry out before watering again. Reduce watering through winter.

COLD HARDINESS: 25°F (–3.9°C)

PROPAGATION: By seed   **BLOOM TIME:** Summer

Previously known as *Notocactus magnificus*, this is a beautifully geometric cactus. It is a blue-green globe with wool and golden spines along the vertical ribs, and it can be found growing singly or in large clustering mounds in time. Bright lemon-yellow flowers appear at the very top in summer. In its homeland, balloon cactus grows in hilly grasslands and on walls between cracks in the rocks or in the shade of larger growing plants. It grows in one of the most temperate regions of Brazil, with warm and cool seasons, and often temperatures will fall to just above freezing without harming the plants, because the locale is also very arid. The soil there is well drained and has a fairly high organic content. Water with caution in winter, as it can lose its roots if the soil stays cold and wet for extended periods.

Peperomia graveolens

RUBY GLOW PEPEROMIA

FAMILY: Piperaceae   **ORIGIN:** Ecuador

CULTURE: Needs very porous soil with excellent drainage and very bright light to filtered sun. Water thoroughly when dry, but allow to dry somewhat inbetween. Protect from frost.

COLD HARDINESS: 35°F (1.7°C)   **PROPAGATION:** By cuttings

BLOOM TIME: Summer

This plant is a high-altitude forest dweller and a favorite houseplant. The stems and undersides of the V-shaped leaves are a beautiful wine red, and the upper sides are green with a "window" in the top. The red coloration absorbs the reflected green light of the forest floor for photosynthesis, while the top green surface and the window take in the direct sunlight from above. When flowering, it will produce spikes held that are covered with microscopic cream or white flowers. They have an unpleasant odor, hence the name *graveolens*, which literally means "heavy-smelling" or, more appropriately, "rank."

Pleiospilos nelii

SPLIT ROCK

FAMILY: Aizoaceae

ORIGIN: South Africa

CULTURE: Needs very porous soil with excellent drainage and full to part sun. Water thoroughly during the warmer months, allowing the soil to dry slightly before repeating. Reduce water in winter and protect from frost.

COLD HARDINESS: 25°F (−3.9°C)

PROPAGATION: By seed

BLOOM TIME: Spring

Being a member of the group of succulents known as "mimicry plants," *Pleiospilos nelii* has evolved to imitate its surroundings by looking not unlike a rock or stone. The extremely succulent pair of grayish green leaves form a cleft egg shape, which can grow quite large, up to 4" (10.2 cm) in diameter. As a new pair of leaves emerges from the center, the two outer leaves deflate, putting their moisture back into the new growth. It has silky, golden-apricot flowers with white centers that are unusually large for the size of the plant. There is a purple-colored variety known as 'Royal Flush'.

Plumeria rubra

PLUMERIA, FRANGIPANI

FAMILY: Apocynaceae

ORIGIN: Mexico, Central America, Colombia, Venezuela

CULTURE: Needs full sun with porous, well-draining soil. Water regularly spring to fall. Keep on the dry side in winter, watering only occasionally, and protect from frost.

COLD HARDINESS: 35°F (1.7°C)

PROPAGATION: By cuttings

BLOOM TIME: Summer to fall

The Central American heritage of *Plumeria* is nearly unknown, with its introduction to other tropical regions, such as Southeast Asia, India, Australia, and especially Tahiti and Hawaii, where its flowers are made into the ubiquitous floral lei. Plants grow as spreading shrubs to small trees 5' to 25' (1.5 m to 7.6 m) tall and wide. Leaves are large, dark green, and oval, ringing the tips of the succulent branches that display clusters of intoxicatingly fragrant five-petal flowers. White and yellow are typical flower colors but hybridizing with related species has now created many shades of pink, red, and even tricolored. As temperatures begin to cool in the fall, *Plumeria* go deciduous and dormant. They need very little water all winter until leafing out again in spring. A combination of cold and wet often leads to plants rotting during this time.

Portulacaria afra

ELEPHANT'S FOOD, ELEPHANT BUSH, SPEKBOOM

FAMILY: Portulacaceae

ORIGIN: Eastern Cape of South Africa, Mozambique

CULTURE: Needs full sun with porous, well-draining soil. Water regularly spring to fall, allowing the soil to dry between applications. Keep on the dry side in winter, watering only occasionally.

COLD HARDINESS: 25° to 30°F (–3.9° to –1.1°C)

PROPAGATION: By cuttings

BLOOM TIME: Summer

In its native habitat, *Portulacaria afra* forms large thickets known in the Afrikaans language as *spekboomvelds*. Elephants see these thickets of their favorite food as a buffet and it can provide up to 80 percent of their diet. A group of elephants can quickly strip all the leaves and smaller branches in a single feeding. Quick to bounce back, the plants will have regrown lush new greenery in as little as 2 weeks. Stocky 3" (7.6 cm)-diameter trunks support a framework of mahogany-colored lateral branches, with an overall mature height of 8' to 12' (2.4 to 3.7 m). Rounded, very succulent, emerald-green leaves are the perfect accent to the red-brown branches. In summer, small clusters of sweetly fragrant, tiny lilac to purple flowers are an unexpected surprise. In relatively frost-free locations, this is an excellent landscape plant for containers and patios or for use as a privacy screen. It has also become a favorite succulent for bonsai treatment.

Sansevieria trifasciata 'Laurentii'
SNAKE PLANT, MOTHER-IN-LAW'S TONGUE, BOWSTRING HEMP

FAMILY: Asparagaceae　**ORIGIN:** Tropical West Africa

CULTURE: Needs very porous, well-draining soil with bright light to filtered sun. Water thoroughly, allowing soil to dry out before watering again, and protect from frost.

COLD HARDINESS: 35°F (1.7°C)

PROPAGATION: By division, leaf cuttings

BLOOM TIME: Summer to fall

One of the common names, bowstring hemp, most likely is from the USDA's attempt to grow the species as a fiber replacement for cannabis in the early part of the last century. This tropical plant forms clumps of erect, sword-shaped, deep green leaves with pale green transverse bands. The small, tubular, pale green flowers are on a stiff spike and have a pleasant fragrance. They often go unnoticed, being hidden among the taller clumps of upright leaves. This is an excellent indoor houseplant with lower light requirements compared to most succulent plants. Do not allow the plant to sit in water, as this may lead to root rot.

Sedum morganianum 'Burrito'
BURRO'S TAIL

FAMILY: Crassulaceae　**ORIGIN:** Mexico, Honduras

CULTURE: Needs very porous, well-draining soil with very bright light to filtered sun. Water thoroughly, allowing soil to almost dry out before watering again, and protect from frost.

COLD HARDINESS: 35°F (1.7°C)

PROPAGATION: By cuttings, leaves　**BLOOM TIME:** Rarely

This grows well outside (in frost-free areas) or indoors in very bright light or filtered sun but not extreme heat. It does well with moderate watering all year, except in winter, when it should be infrequently watered. Excess water can damage the plant in a short time. The leaf structure is fragile and will readily break off the stem when manipulated. The leaves will stay alive for many days and roots will emerge after a few days. Protect from frost. 'Burrito' (which means "little burro") is a select cultivar of the regular species *Morganianum* and has smaller, shorter, and fatter leaves compared to the usual burro's tail.

Sedum praealtum

BUSH SEDUM, BUSH STONECROP

FAMILY: Crassulaceae   **ORIGIN:** Mexico

CULTURE: Needs loose, well-draining soil and full sun. Water thoroughly, allowing the soil to dry slightly before watering again. Enjoys supplemental water in the hottest months but requires little to none in winter.

COLD HARDINESS: 20°F (–6.7°C)

PROPAGATION: By cuttings, leaves   **BLOOM TIME:** Spring

This is an unusual sedum in that, unlike most all others, it grows as a small sub-shrub rather than a creeping groundcover. Freely branching, the tangle of sturdy stems provide support to one another, allowing it to grow as an upright mounded shrub to 3' (0.9 m) tall and wide with time. The leaves form bright green, loose rosettes at the stem ends, looking similar to an Aeonium. In the landscape, it can be used in street medians and other locations where a low-growing, low-maintenance, drought-resistant plant is needed. Masses of bright yellow, star-shaped flowers cover the plant in spring.

Sedum rubrotinctum

PORK AND BEANS, CHRISTMAS CHEER STONECROP, JELLY BEANS

FAMILY: Crassulaceae   **ORIGIN:** Mexico

CULTURE: Needs loose, well-draining soil and full sun to light shade. Water thoroughly, allowing the soil to dry slightly before watering again. Enjoys supplemental water in the hottest months but requires little to none in winter.

COLD HARDINESS: 25°F (–3.9°C)

PROPAGATION: By cuttings, leaves   **BLOOM TIME:** Summer

This is a familiar succulent classic that works well as a small area groundcover and certainly as a filler in rock gardens. The slowly trailing stems reach 8" to 10" (20.3 to 25.4 cm) long and are covered with gleaming green jelly bean leaves tipped in cherry-red. Don't be tempted by the candy-like appeal, though. *Sedum rubrotinctum* is not edible and may cause irritation when ingested or touched. Stress from excess sun, heat, cold, or drought intensifies the color. Too little sun and the stems grow long and stretched, losing their compact look and signature color and becoming just an unremarkable green. *S. rubrotinctum variegata* 'Aurora' is a beautiful cultivar that is a pale whitish green infused with light pink and darker pink tips.

Sedum rupestre 'Angelina'

'ANGELINA' STONECROP

FAMILY: Crassulaceae   **ORIGIN:** Europe

CULTURE: Needs full sun, well-draining porous soil, and thorough watering, allowing the soil to dry before repeating. Reduce water in winter.

COLD HARDINESS: 35°F (1.7°C)

PROPAGATION: By cuttings, leaves   **BLOOM TIME:** Summer

The type species (particular species on which the description of a genus is based), *Sedum rupestre*, is plain green. The cultivar 'Angelina' was found as a sport growing in a private garden in Croatia and named in honor of the owner. Unlike the species, it is a bright yellow, especially when grown in full sun; with stress in fall as temperatures begin to drop, it takes on a very attractive orange blush. This is a very tough stonecrop with extreme cold hardiness and drought tolerance. It does look better with occasional watering in the hottest months and locations. Rapidly growing, it makes a suitable small area groundcover and can be used as a trailing, cascading plant in hanging baskets and containers. Lower light conditions will cause it to lose its brilliance and become primarily green.

Sedum spathulifolium 'Capo Blanco'

SPOON LEAF STONECROP

FAMILY: Crassulaceae

ORIGIN: North American Pacific Northwest

CULTURE: Needs full sun and well-draining soil with occasional watering in the hotter months, but must be kept on the dry side in winter. Cold, wet soil encourages root rot.

COLD HARDINESS: −15°F (−26.1°C)

PROPAGATION: By cuttings   **BLOOM TIME:** Summer

A well-behaved species, 'Capo Blanco' leaves form tight rosettes that are covered in a heavy, powdery, silvery-white coating. In cooler weather, the green coloring underneath takes on a dark purple hue that looks particularly attractive combined with the silvery powder coat. As an added bonus, clusters of tiny yellow flowers contrast nicely with the foliage in summer. This is a great choice for a groundcover, container, rock garden, or pathway accent, because it stays compact and low growing at around 3" (7.6 cm) tall and spreading to 12" (30.5 cm). It is fairly cold hardy, but remember to keep the soil dry in winter to avoid root rot.

Sempervivum arachnoideum

COBWEB HOUSELEEK, SPIDER WEB HENS AND CHICKS

FAMILY: Crassulaceae   **ORIGIN:** Southern Europe

CULTURE: Needs full sun to light shade and shade protection in very hot, sunny locations. Prefers a sandy, well-draining soil and requires little watering once established.

COLD HARDINESS: −25°F (−31.7°C)

PROPAGATION: By offsets   **BLOOM TIME:** Spring to summer

The name for the genus comes from the Latin words *semper*, meaning "always," and *vivus*, meaning "living," in reference to the long-living nature of these plants. Spider web hens and chicks forms hardy, compact rosettes that have small white threads running back and forth across the face and bears an uncanny resemblance to a spider's web building. The short bloom stalks that appear spring to summer display beautifully exotic, star-shaped, magenta flowers. Historically, it was thought to have mysterious abilities to ward off evil and protect a house from lightning strikes. As such, it was planted outside of dwelling entrances and used on the thatched roofs of Europe. It is a perfect plant for growing in crevices of stone walls and rocky outcroppings.

Senecio articulatus 'Variegatus'

VARIEGATED CANDLE PLANT

FAMILY: Asteraceae   **ORIGIN:** South Africa

CULTURE: Needs filtered sun or light shade and very porous, well-draining soil. A winter grower, it takes occasional watering at that time and water should be reduced to even less in warmer months. Protect from frost.

COLD HARDINESS: 35°F (1.7°C)

PROPAGATION: By cuttings   **BLOOM TIME:** Summer to fall

Variegated candle plant is a wonderfully unusual-looking succulent. It is comprised of short sausage-like as well as round stem segments, reaching an overall height of 1' to 2' (0.3 to 0.6 m) tall with some branching. Erect but supple stems are green with a light green pattern, and the leaves exhibit exotic combinations of white, green, cream, pink, and purple variegation. Being a winter grower, it is leafless most of the rest of the year and exists as simple, swollen stems. Care problems can be caused by the urge to water during the summer dormancy period, when watering should really be reduced to a bare minimum. Rotting becomes very likely under this type of regime.

Senecio talinoides var. mandraliscae

BLUE CHALK STICKS

FAMILY: Asteraceae   **ORIGIN:** South Africa

CULTURE: Needs full sun and porous, well-draining soil. Provide thorough watering, allowing the soil to dry before repeating, and reduce water in winter. Looks best with supplemental watering during the hottest months and in inland areas.

COLD HARDINESS: 20°F (−6.7°C)

PROPAGATION: By cuttings   **BLOOM TIME:** Summer

This is an excellent ice plant–type trailing groundcover. Its most noticeable feature is the glowing blue-gray succulent foliage. Leaves like blue fingers stand upright on trailing stems that spread outward to 3' (0.9 m) in length. Like most senecios, it produces white to tan powder puff–type flowers that are relatively unremarkable. The noteworthy blue color of the fingers creates a breathtaking contrast in the garden when combined with other dark-colored succulents, such as *Aeonium* 'Zwartkop'.

Senecio scaposus

SILVER CORAL

FAMILY: Asteraceae   **ORIGIN:** South Africa

CULTURE: Prefers full sun to light shade and very porous, well-draining soil. Water thoroughly, allowing the soil to dry out before watering again. Water only enough to keep from shriveling in winter.

COLD HARDINESS: 25°F (−3.9°C)

PROPAGATION: By cuttings   **BLOOM TIME:** Summer

Members of the Senecio family come in all shapes and sizes, and this is a most attractive species with long, dazzling, bright silver-white, succulent finger-like leaves. The leaves are actually covered with a silver-white felt-type skin that may shed over time as the leaves expand, exposing solid green. The felt-like coating serves as protection against the harsh sun in its native habitat. This is a short-stemmed shrublet that branches at the base and can make a 1'- (0.3 m) tall mound. The unusual finger-like leaves resemble a sea anemone or finger coral, making it a favorite to use when planting a faux "undersea-themed" succulent garden. Showy yellow daisy flowers appear in summer.

Stapelia gigantea

CARRION FLOWER, AFRICAN STARFISH FLOWER

FAMILY: Apocynaceae   **ORIGIN:** Tropical and southern Africa

CULTURE: Grow in full sun to light shade in hottest, inland locations. Needs porous, well-draining soil. Water occasionally, allowing the soil to dry slightly before watering again. Keep on the dry side in winter, watering only enough to avoid shriveling, and protect from frost.

COLD HARDINESS: 30°F (–1.1°C)

PROPAGATION: By cuttings   **BLOOM TIME:** Late summer–fall

Listed among plants with the worst-smelling flowers, this member of the milkweed family sports one of the largest flowers in the plant kingdom. Huge, balloon-like buds open to amazing (10"- to 16" [25.4 to 40.6 cm]-wide) perfect five-point stars. Pale yellow-ochre and decorated with thin, narrow maroon bars, the flowers exude the infamous aroma of rotting flesh like other members of the Stapelia clan. The unpleasant fragrance is the mechanism for attracting its main pollinator—flies. The upright pale green stems are four sided and 6" to 12" (15.3 to 30.5 cm) tall, taking on a red-purple hue in extreme sun exposure. Plants spread outward 18" to 24" (45.7 to 61 cm) on creeping stems and can make an interesting small-scale groundcover in sunny, frost-free locations.

Titanopsis calcarea

JEWEL PLANT, CONCRETE LEAF

FAMILY: Aizoaceae

ORIGIN: South Africa

CULTURE: Grow in full sun to light shade in hottest, inland locations. Needs porous, well-draining soil. Water occasionally, allowing the soil to dry slightly before watering again. Keep on the dry side in summer, watering only enough to avoid shriveling, and protect from frost.

COLD HARDINESS: 25°F (–3.9°C)

PROPAGATION: By seed, division

BLOOM TIME: Fall to winter

Titanopsis is another fascinating member of the group known as "mimicry" plants that physically blend in and "mimic" their habitat. Coming from a coarse sand and pebble environment, the plant features leaves tipped with numerous wart-like bumps that are a variety of subtle colors and look like the surrounding sandy soil. The leaves are also actually very hard to the touch, feeling almost stone-like. This is a winter grower, receiving the bulk of its water at that time and preferring to stay quite dry from spring through summer, with only an occasional drink to keep it from shriveling. Bright yellow, daisy-like flowers, large for the size of the plant, appear in fall and winter. This is one of the more easily grown mimicry plants as long as it doesn't get overwatered.

Trichocereus grandiflorus Hybrids

TORCH CACTUS

FAMILY: Cactaceae

ORIGIN: Argentina

CULTURE: Needs full sun, well-draining porous soil, and thorough watering, allowing the soil to dry before repeating. Reduce water in winter.

COLD HARDINESS: 15°F (−9.4°C)

PROPAGATION: By offsets

BLOOM TIME: Summer

Torch cactuses form a clumping colony, with stems to 15" (38.1 cm) in height. The species is known for its beautiful, clear red flowers to 4" (10.2 cm) in diameter. Over the years, the species has been continuously hybridized, resulting in a vast array of colors, including yellow, gold, white, pink, light pink with rose mid-stripes, orange, red, and purple; some are even bicolored. In many cases, the flower size has been increased as well to 9" (22.9 cm) in diameter, competing with *Epiphyllum*, or "orchid cactuses," for their outlandish size and colors. They respond dramatically to generous water and fertilizer. With weekly watering and monthly feeding, the best cultivars will respond with blooms biweekly or so for three months and longer. Through hybridization, the actual appearance of the plant has changed as well. Compared to the slenderer species type, many newer hybrids have thick, cylindrical bodies to 10" (25.4 cm) in diameter, with offsets forming clumps or colonies that span several feet across. A mass group like this is breathtaking when in bloom, with dozens of large, brightly colored trumpets all open together. Blooming can continue on and off in flushes over several weeks.

Trichocereus pachanoi/Echinopsis pachanoi

SAN PEDRO CACTUS

FAMILY: Cactaceae

ORIGIN: Peru, Ecuador, Bolivia, Argentina

CULTURE: Grow in full sun with porous, well-draining soil. Water regularly spring to fall, allowing soil to dry slightly between applications. Keep on the dry side in winter, watering only occasionally.

COLD HARDINESS: 15°F (–9.4°C)

PROPAGATION: By seed, cuttings

BLOOM TIME: Summer

The San Pedro cactus is a resident of the higher altitudes of the Andes in the northernmost part of South America. This is an area of somewhat regular high rainfall in the spring and summer months. Because of this, in culture it can be watered much more regularly than most cactuses during this time and is a relatively fast grower. Speed of growth is also increased by feeding monthly during this growing season with a balanced, all-purpose fertilizer. Growth is columnar and can reach 18' (5.5 m) tall. Established plants with this kind of care can grow 1' (0.3 m) a year. It can sunburn in extremely hot summer locations, so light shade is recommended. Stop feeding by the end of summer and reduce watering in fall to initiate winter dormancy. It will only need occasional water in winter. This is a night bloomer with large, white, fragrant flowers. Aside from being a statuesque landscape plant, it is one of several cactuses grown for its psychoactive properties. Archeological studies have found evidence of use going back 2,000 years, to Moche culture in Peru.

Index

About the Authors

JOHN BAGNASCO has been an integral part of the gardening industry for more than 45 years, starting with a degree in horticultural marketing (from Michigan State University) and followed by a decade at Frank's Nursery and Crafts in Detroit. He moved to California to become regional manager and buyer for the Nurseryland division of Sunbelt Nursery Group and then became the head buyer for Armstrong Garden Centers based in Glendora, California. John joined Creative Promotions in October 2000 as a senior magazine editor and radio personality for *Garden Compass*. He is currently the president and co-host of the nationally syndicated "Garden America Radio Show," which reaches 1.1 million listeners every weekend. He is also the president of www.GardenTube.com, a YouTube–type site for gardeners, and is a managing partner in SuperNaturals Grafted Vegetables, LLC. John has taught horticulture classes and is a rose breeder who introduced more than a dozen new varieties. He was host of the DVD *The Essential Guide to Roses*. John's other books include *Planting Designs for Cactus and Succulents* and *Plants for the Home*, Vol I.

BOB REIDMULLER is a lifelong, hands-on plant geek, beginning from a young age under the tutelage of his grandfather in New Jersey. A family relocation to Southern California at the age of 16 offered a plethora of horticultural and botanical experiences and opportunities. Starting a small private nursery based primarily on tropical plants, such as staghorn ferns and orchids, led to several years working for Solana Orchids, a large local producer of orchids for the cut-flower market. This path eventually led to over twenty-five years and counting working for Altman Plants in Vista, California, the nation's largest wholesale producer of cactuses and succulents. With the phenomenal craze of all things succulent and being on staff as resident horticulturist there, he spends a major part of his time offering cultural information on this fascinating plant group to their wholesale and retail customer base nationwide. This also includes giving talks and facility tours to local garden clubs, schools, and university horticulture groups. He has written articles for various trade publications and was a regular contributor to *Garden Compass Magazine*. He is a frequent guest co-host of the nationally syndicated *Garden America Radio Show*, which reaches 1.1 million listeners every weekend.